Tania Wolski – Luc Vincent

LÉON STYNEN
ARCHITECT

snoeck

TABLE OF CONTENTS

A MAN A FAMILY — 6
Anne Stynen, Tania & Sophie Wolski

THE ARCHITECT — 28

HIS CONTEMPORARIES — 120
Marc Dubois

THE TEACHER & LA CAMBRE — 144
Pablo Lhoas

FORMS & FUNCTIONS — 198
Luc Vincent

ART & THE KURSAAL — 222
Els Degryse

SOUTH ANTWERP AN ENVIRONMENT — 242
Xavier Dewulf

A MAN
A FAMILY

ANNE STYNEN,
TANIA & SOPHIE WOLSKI

In Spain with Anne, 1952

With his wife Marie-Jeanne and his nephew

With his daughter

With his son Philippe, 1936

With his wife an his daughter Anne, Hôtel des Trois Rois, Bâle, Switzerland

Writing about my father is not easy – there's so much to tell.

He was a man of integrity: honest, hard-working, severe and demanding as much of himself as of others. With him, nothing was left to chance. But his passion for architecture counted above everything else and his desire to communicate it was great. This remained so until the end of his life. I remember young architecture students coming to the house and how he recounted to them episodes of his career as an architect – his joys, his sorrows, the people he had known and met. His great wish was to integrate the visual arts into architecture. During his time as director of the Institut d'architecture de La Cambre, he therefore invited a number of artists, architects and others to take part in workshops and give lectures. He was keen to bring to the school founded by Henry van de Velde – whom he esteemed, respected and often visited at his home in Switzerland – the influence it deserved. The institute was his darling child. He did everything he could to help it obtain university status, something which happened after he left!

For his granddaughters, he was a sweet grandfather. He adored them and spent moments with them that were unforgettable, both for them and for him. He was not an easy man to live with, but what we got from him was fabulous. At his house on Lake Garda, he loved to bring his friends over. He would show them around, either by car or in his motor boat, and spend long evenings on the terrace, facing the lake with a good glass of grappa. He liked to spoil his wife, his daughter (me) and his granddaughters. His generosity was immense.

He took us all around Italy, which he was in love with, often including in the party our Santina, the housekeeper of his 'paradise' on the lake. I adored my father, even if I sometimes suffered under his authority. It was stronger than him; my mother also did not find it easy. But he had so many qualities that they erased everything else.

There are many anecdotes to tell about him. He made us laugh until we cried, but his seriousness quickly took over. He often said that his character had changed after the death of his son, which he often talked about. Although it remained an open wound throughout his whole life, he never imposed the weight of this suffering on us.

Let me add one more thing before finishing: his gratitude was eternal to those who helped him. One episode still sticks in my memory. In 1945, at the end of the war, the first thing he did was buy a second-hand car, an Imperia convertible. And off we went to France. Both he and my mother were keen to thank the couple who had hosted us during the exodus of 1940 – the phoney war. At the time, Dad took us in his car – not yet requisitioned by the Germans – and headed for France. We stopped at Trie-Château, in the Oise. He rang the doorbell of a large house and asked the gentleman who opened the door if he could leave us at his house for a few days. He said that he would come back to get us as soon as possible. The response was immediate: 'From this moment, your wife and your daughter are part of my family.' He would never forget this. We often returned to Trie-Château.

I miss my father a lot. I will never forget him. He was my pillar. I was able to count on him all my life.

ANNE STYNEN

New-York, 1939

Elsdonck private residence during building, Antwerp, 1933, Léon Stynen with his son on the left

Chandigarh, 1963

You're sitting across the table from me. Resting on the white porcelain plate on the light green linen tablecloth is an orange, just like every morning. I observe the precision with which you separate each quarter with your small fork and knife.

Your love of detail and precision – everywhere, always.

A little black wooden mouse with a long moustache and a brown breastplate… He's always there on your big white table, next to your pencils, erasers, rulers, compasses and graph paper. I watch you use them as you talk to me: you explain to me lines, shapes, proportions, space, light; you introduce me to architecture; you give me a taste for aesthetics.

There's passion in everything you do.

Your overcoat – that's what you call a coat in your grandfather vocabulary – your hat, your suit, your bow tie and your black leather shoes – always impeccably polished. And off we go to discover the world. Museums, churches, castles, palaces… Everything comes alive, becomes captivating. History and architecture, intertwined in your words, are constant features of our walks. You detail the architectural styles, their eras, their techniques and their specific beauties.
Sophie and I listen to you religiously, without interrupting, and then ask a thousand questions, which you love to answer.
Your pleasure in transmitting what touches you, both emotionally and academically.

What a source of inspiration for our young imagination! We transform it into all kinds of different creations, which you encourage without limits.
You were a loving grandfather above all!

I wake up to the sound of the splashing waves breaking against the walls. I leave my room, cross the two metres that separate me from the water of Lake Garda, lapping the house you built there for the family.
Your haven, without frills, in direct contact with the elements.
My taste buds discover the flavours of the two house cooks: pappardelle with ceps by Angelina, pizzas by Santina. I walk round the garden and breathe in the lavender, thyme and bay leaves that Nonna has planted with the help of Rino, the gardener.
Your sense of humanity and respect for everyone, whoever they are.

It's impossible to think of you without thinking of Nonna, your wife, our grandmother – a great traveller and a great reader. She tells us her exciting and often hilarious stories. She draws, she writes poems, acrostics, stories and, often, your speeches. Bon-Papa and Nonna, Nonna and Bon-Papa, an inseparable duo.

After dinner, I watch the adults sip your grappa, the one you offer your guests. You love sharing it so much with them in this haven of your imagination. I grew up in your generosity and the magic of your architecture, which emerges here from water and light.

Your pleasure at sharing life with others is simple and yet magnified by your creations.

You gave us a taste for freedom, authenticity, humanism and creativity.
Precious gifts that every day remind me of how lucky I am to be your granddaughter.
From wherever you are today – is there an Olympus for architects? – you should be able to see it.

Thank you, Bon-Papa.

For me, as his granddaughter, Bon-Papa was quite simply an extraordinary grandfather.

Despite his commanding presence, my memories of him are almost all of happy times. I was fortunate to know him for a large part of my life, enabling him to pass on to me his love for beauty, his sense of duty and his moral integrity – all of which still accompany me to this day.

My memories of my maternal family are partly linked to the houses – each one built by Léon Stynen – that we were lucky enough to live in.

When I think of him, a myriad of feelings surface, taking me back to a distant past. Our holiday departures for Lake Garda were organized down to the minute. Nothing was left to chance – neither the order in which the suitcases were placed in the car boot, nor the time of departure indicated on his notepad. From that moment on, each stop on the journey – from filling up the car with petrol, to eating in a restaurant and sleeping in a hotel – corresponded to a predefined schedule.

Bon-Papa, just as the architect Léon Stynen, was precise in his everyday life.

I can still see him drinking his aperitif, a Campari, by the lake, under the weeping willow, always in the shade, dressed impeccably in long trousers and a pastel cotton shirt.

I can't help but smile when I recall his perfectly Italianized French, which made his often highly animated discussions with local craftsmen a source of great amusement for us as spectators.

I also remember Bon-Papa at work in his office at his home in Antwerp, where my sister and I sometimes spent the weekend. All the objects, books, magazines were placed in meticulous order, and I remember how he inconspicuously returned all the items that we may have stumbled across to their rightful place. I still remember our first visit to the Louvre, where he was our guide in the department of Egyptian antiquities. Finally, quite simply, I still remember a grandfather who loved to spoil his granddaughters.

SOPHIE WOLSKI

With his granddaughter Tania Wolski

Chenard & Walcker, two doors with Weymann carrosserie, 1928

Imperia TA11 Jupiter, 1940

THE ARCHITECT

LÉON STYNEN

ARCHITECTE

DIRECTEUR HONORAIRE DES ECOLES NATIONALES SUPÉRIEURES

D'ARCHITECTURE ET D'URBANISME D'ANVERS ET DE BRUXELLES

C. HUYSMANSLAAN 85 ANTWERPEN

OPTIEK
VAN BAEL ANTWERPEN
Tentoonstellingslaan 65 Tel. 73548

Personal house with studio, Antwerp, 1932

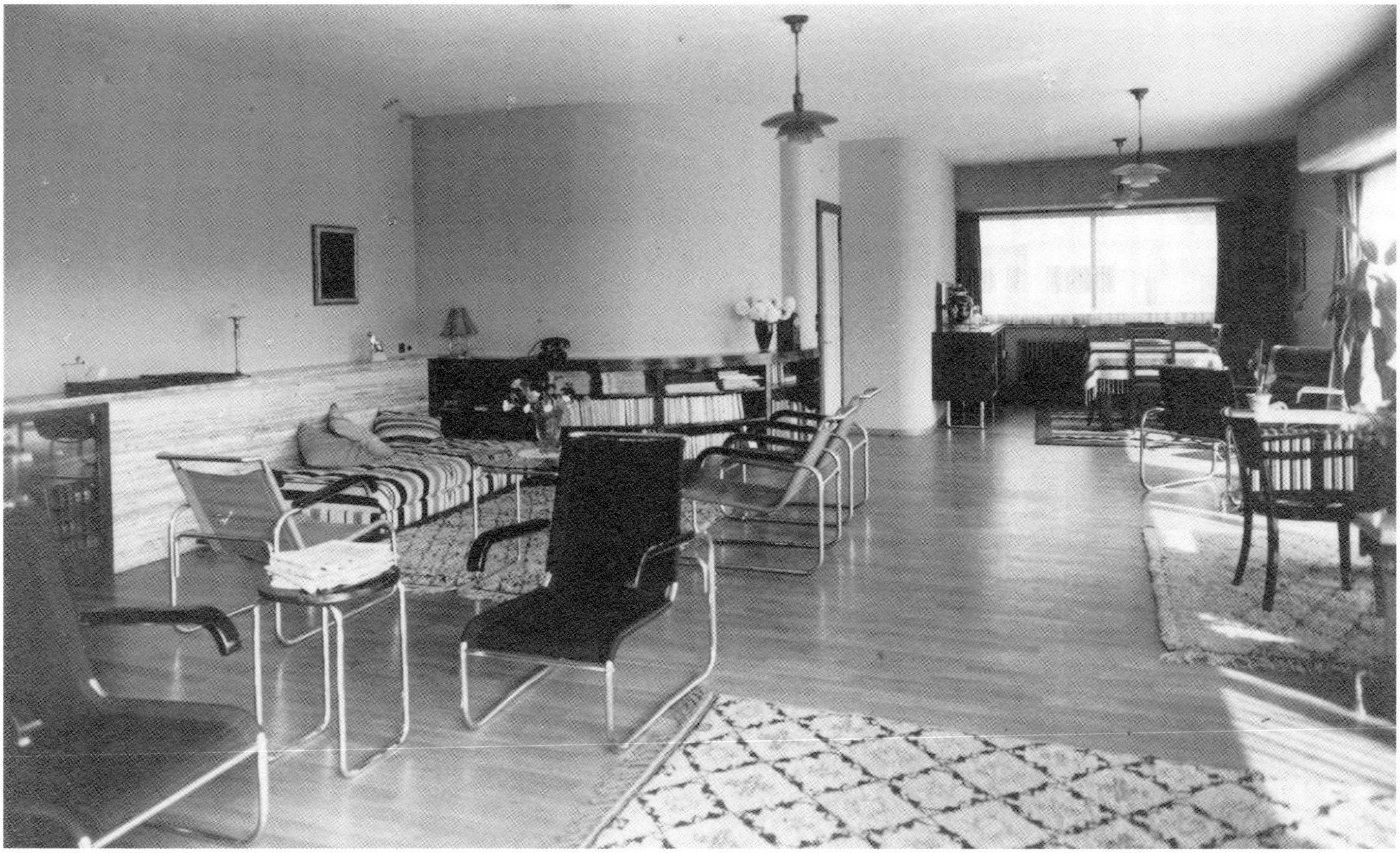

I Tre Cipressi, Gargnano, Lago di Garda, Italy, 1963

43

Stynen-Wolski family home, La Hulpe, 1966

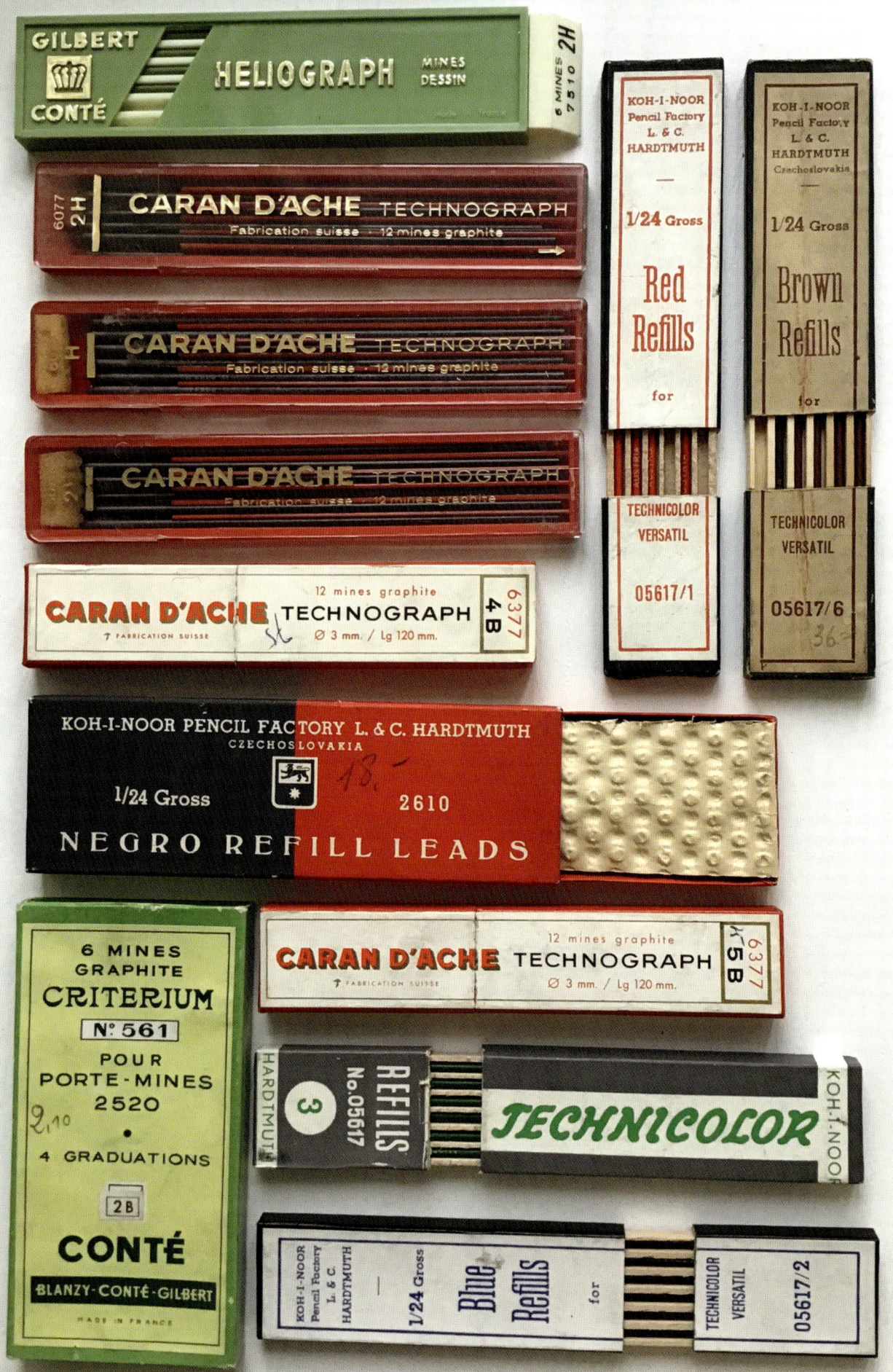

Verstrepen house, Boom, photomontage by Léon Stynen, 1927–28

Antwerp World's Fair, Decorative Arts Pavilion, 1930

Knokke Casino, 1930

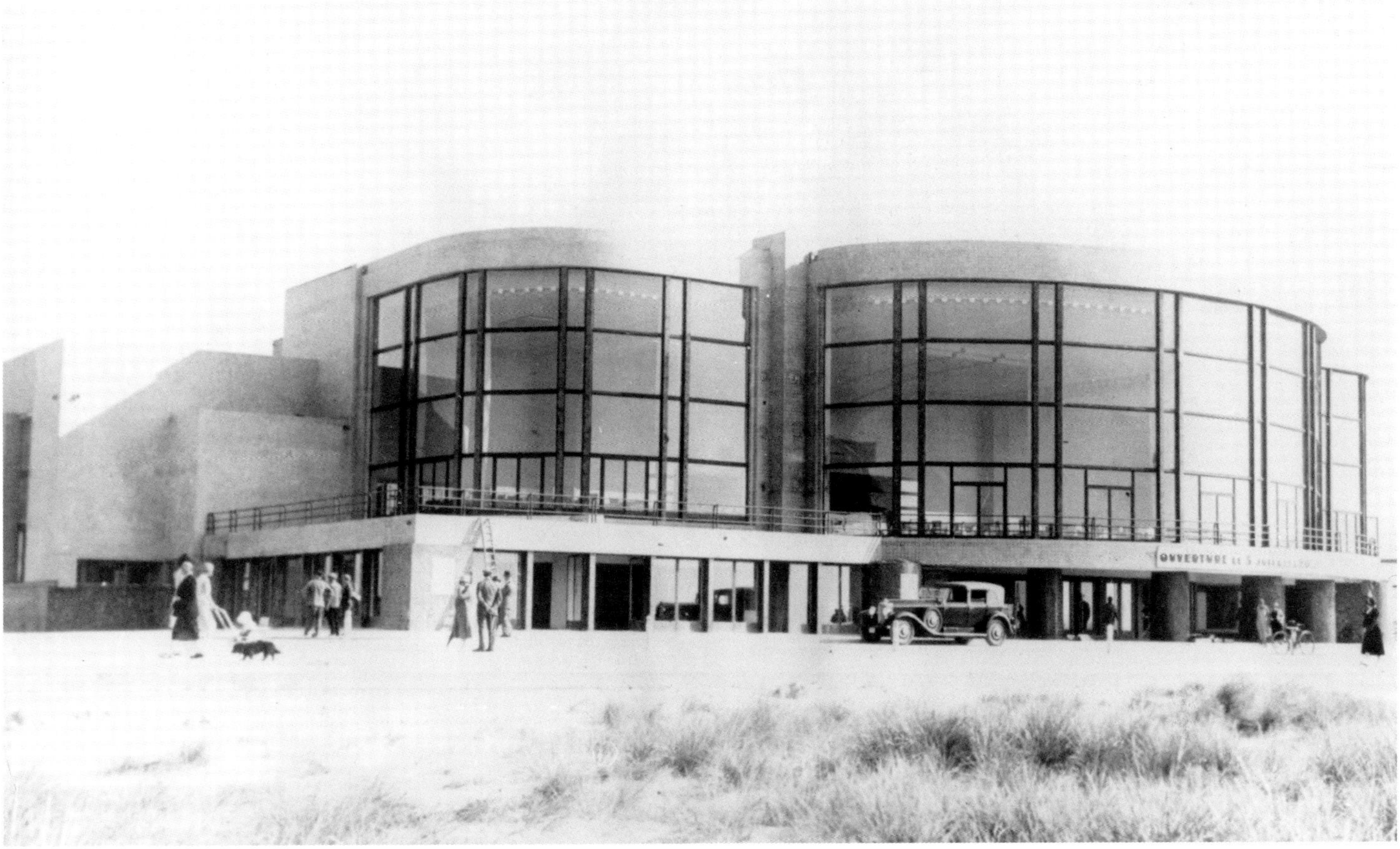

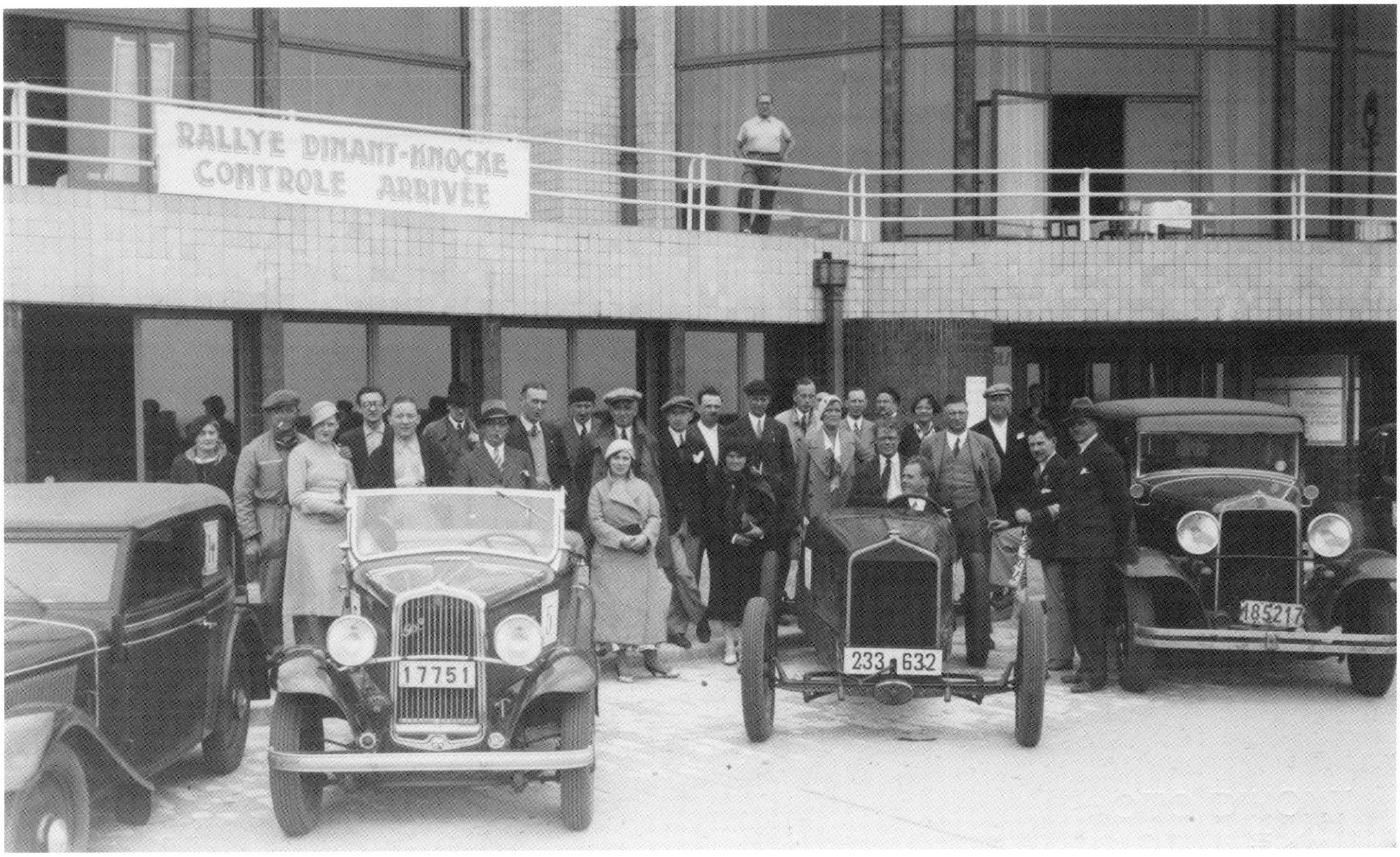
RALLYE DINANT-KNOCKE
CONTROLE ARRIVÉE
17751
233 632
185217

Knokke Casino, 1930

59

Pavilion, Antwerp World's Fair, 1930

Project for Antwerp Institute of Architecture and Urban Planning, 1949

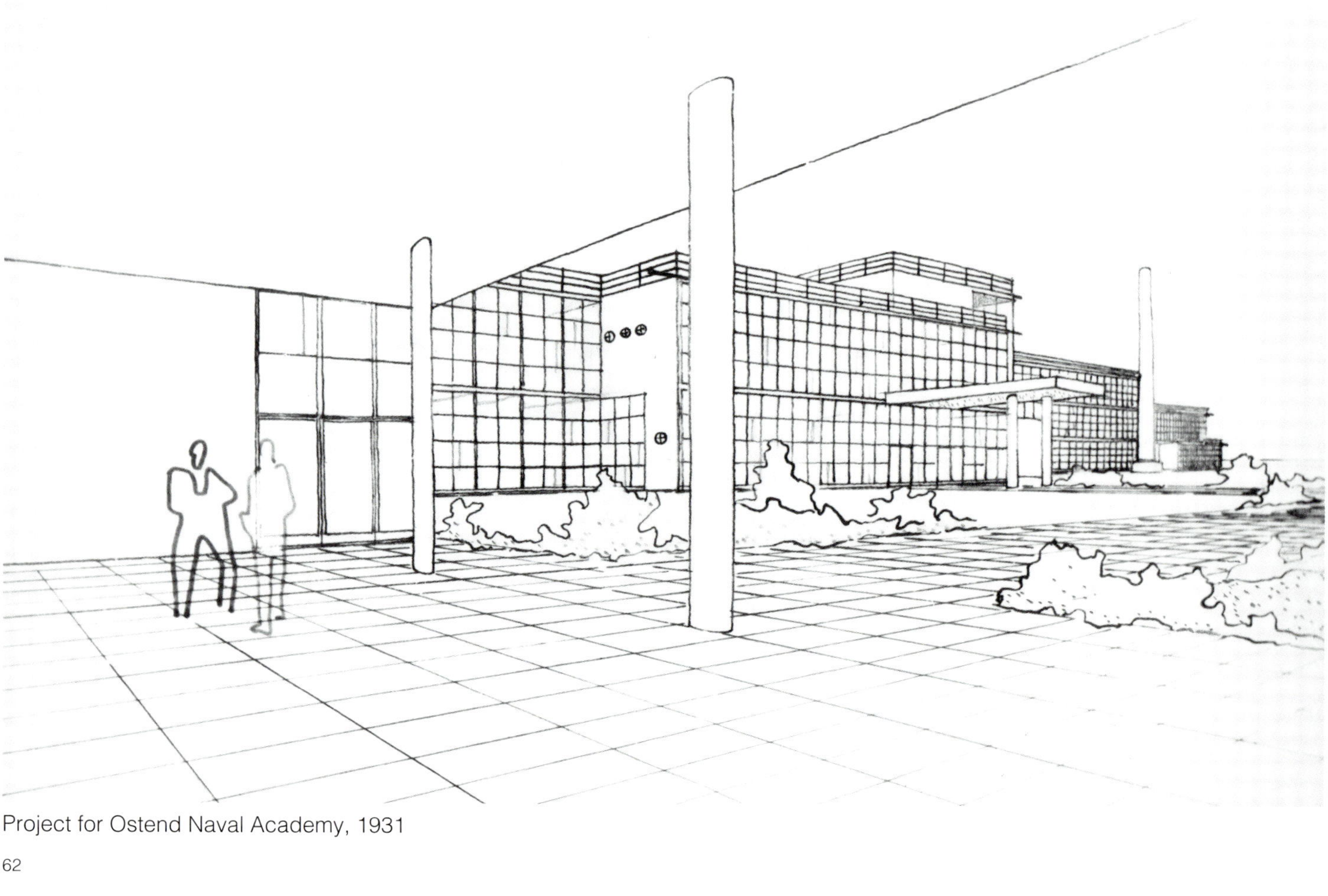

Project for Ostend Naval Academy, 1931

Project (not executed) for Governor's residence, Léopoldville, 1928

INSTITUT NATIONAL BELGE DE RADIO - DIFFUSION
1a, RUE DU BASTION, BRUXELLES

Téléphone 11,47,22 Compte chèque postal 5468
Adresse télégraphique : INR Bruxelles

BELGISCH NATIONAAL INSTITUUT VOOR RADIO-OMROEP
1a, BOLWERKSTRAAT, BRUSSEL

Telefoon 11,47,22 Postcheckrekening 5468
Telegramadres : NIR Brussel

I.N.R. / N.I.R.

9194

N°
Nr d1H/VO.

Direction Générale   **Hoofdbestuur**

RECOMMANDEE.

Le 30 Novembre 1933
Den

Monsieur,

J'ai l'honneur de vous faire savoir que le Conseil de Gestion de l'I.N.R., réuni en séance du 28 Novembre 1933, conformément au règlement du deuxième concours d'architecture pour la construction du bâtiment de l'I.N.R., a fait procéder, par l'huissier Maître VAN HOREN, à l'ouverture des plis contenant le nom des concurrents, plis que cet officier ministériel avait conservé depuis le début des opérations du Jury.

Le Conseil a constaté que le Jury a classé premier et jugé digne d'exécution le projet de M. Joseph DIONGRE, architecte à Uccle.

Le Jury a alloué des primes pour les projets suivants :
ex aequo MM. COPPE Lucien de Woluwe-Saint-Lambert,
DE VESTEL Lucien et COSYNS Max, d'Etterbeek,
PORTIELTJE Alfred, DE BRAYE Jean et STYNEN
Léon d'Anvers,
VAN NUETEN Charles et KEYM Maurice, de
Bruxelles.

A chacun de ces 4 projets, le jury a alloué une prime de dix mille francs.

ex aequo : MM. BLOMME Adrien et BLOMME Ivan de Bruxelles,
de LIGNE Jean et HENDRICKX Jean de Bruxelles.

A chacun de ces deux projets, le jury a alloué une prime de cinq mille francs.

Monsieur Léon STYNEN,
85, Avenue des Colonies
ANVERS.

I. N. R. - N. I. R.

Suite de lettre N° 1.
Vervolg brief Nr

Du 30 Novembre 1933
Van den

91947

Le classement a été déterminé en considérant à la fois la valeur architecturale et les qualités techniques des projets.

Le Conseil de Gestion a entériné le classement du jury et a décidé de confier l'exécution du bâtiment à M. Joseph DIONGRE.

Une exposition des travaux des architectes sera organisée ultérieurement.

Je vous prie, en conséquence, de vouloir bien passer à la comptabilité de l'I.N.R., 1a, rue du Bastion, à partir du 15 décembre, pour toucher la prime qui vous est attribuée, de concert avec vos associés et, à défaut, muni de leur procuration dûment légalisée.

LE DIRECTEUR GÉNÉRAL

Project for the INR building, Place Flagey, Brussels, 1933

PORTIELJE — DE BRAEY — STYNEN.
ARCHITECTES. ANVERS.

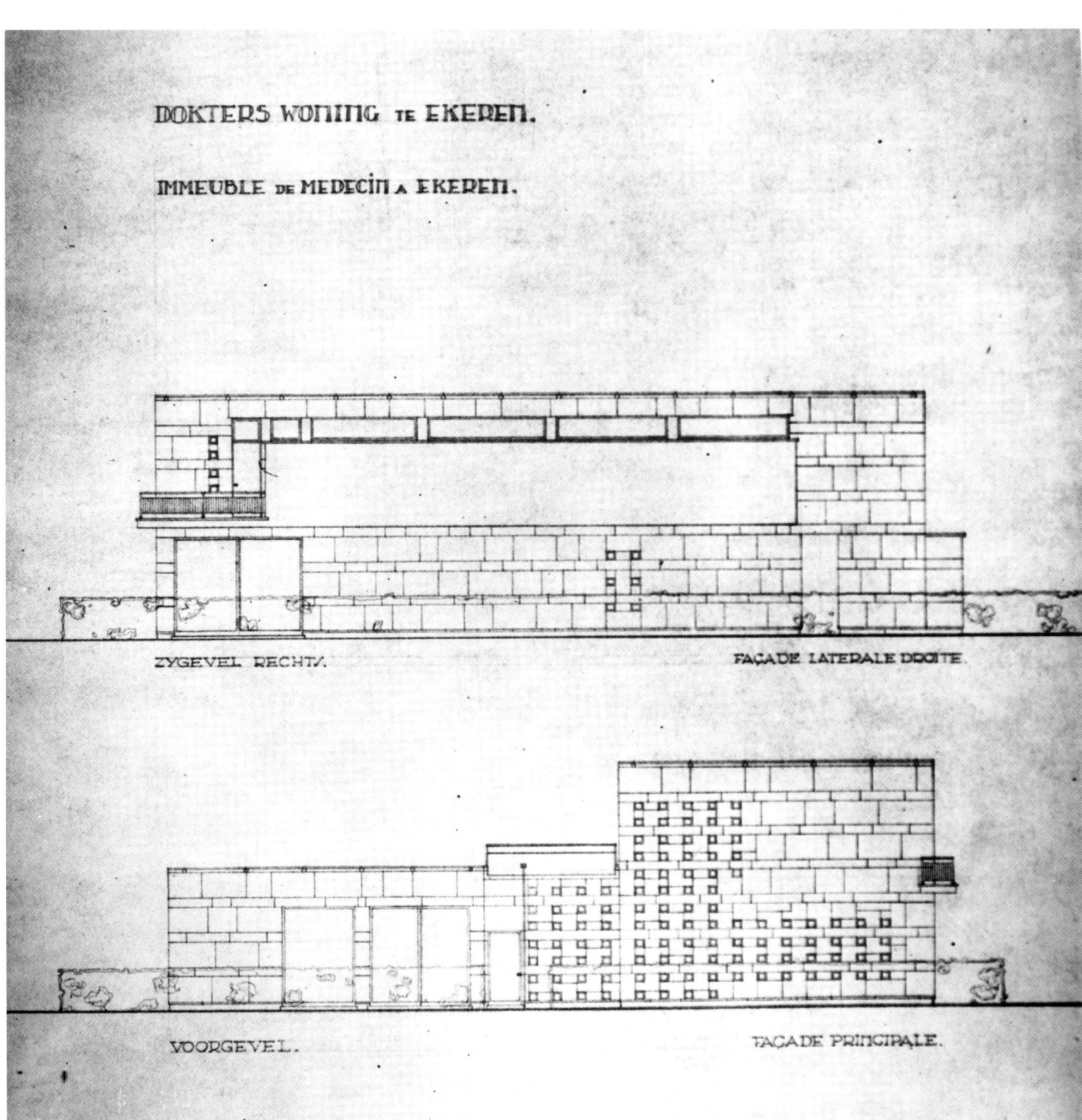

Van Thillo residence, Ekeren, photomontages by Léon Stynen, 1936

Housing complex, Antwerp, 1937

Chaudfontaine Casino, 1938

With Victor Bourgeois and Henri van de Velde, New York, 1939

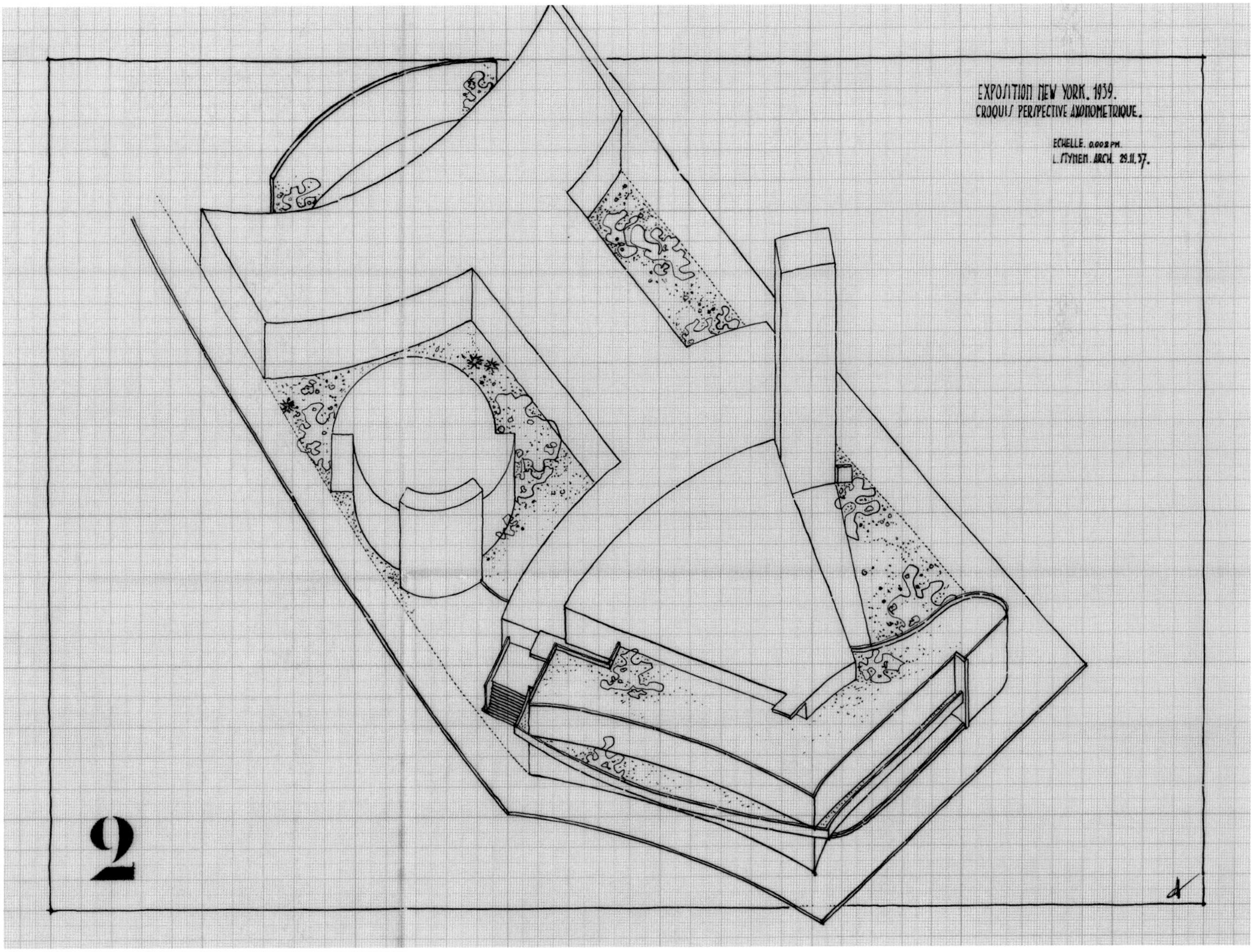

NEW-YORK WORLD'S FAIR
BELGIAN SECTION

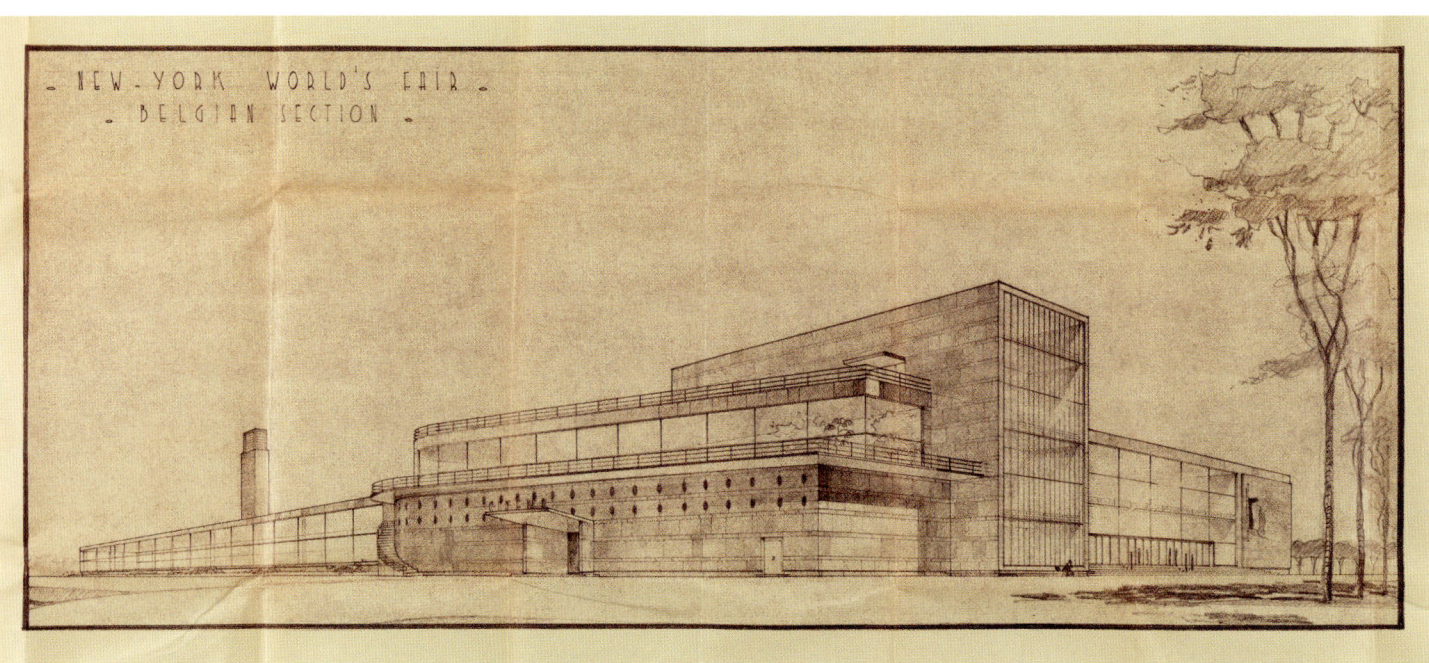

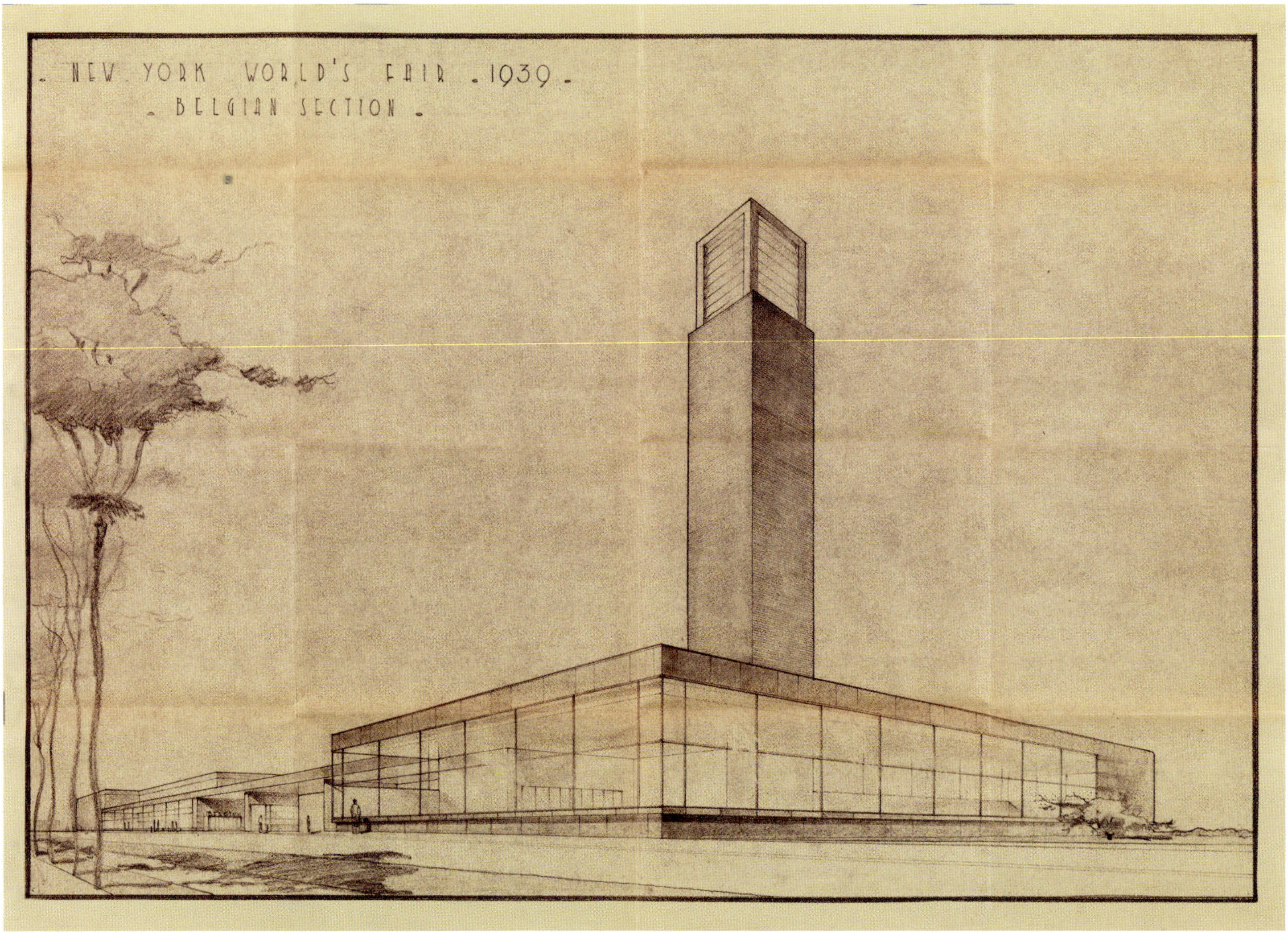
NEW YORK WORLD'S FAIR 1939
BELGIAN SECTION

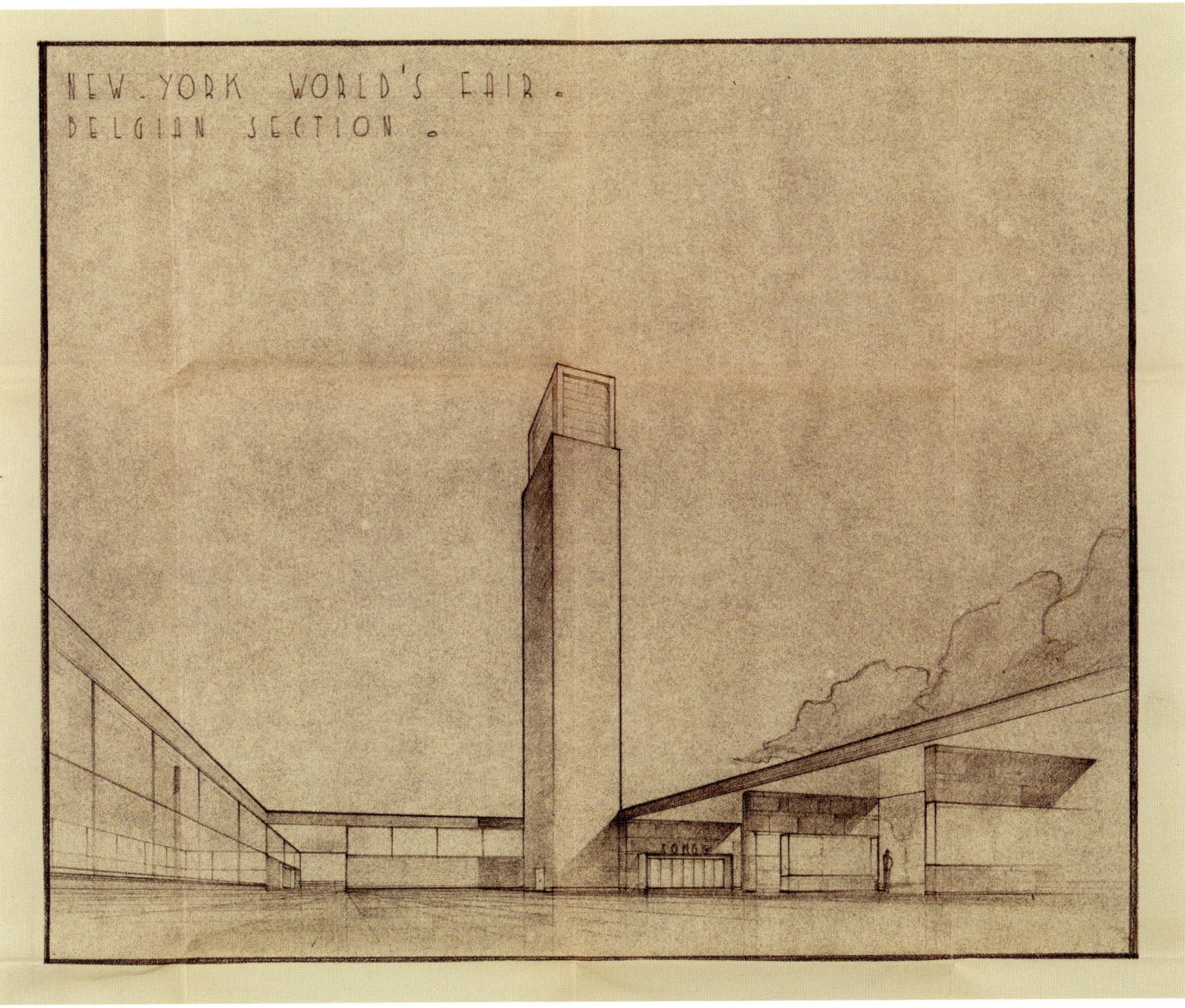

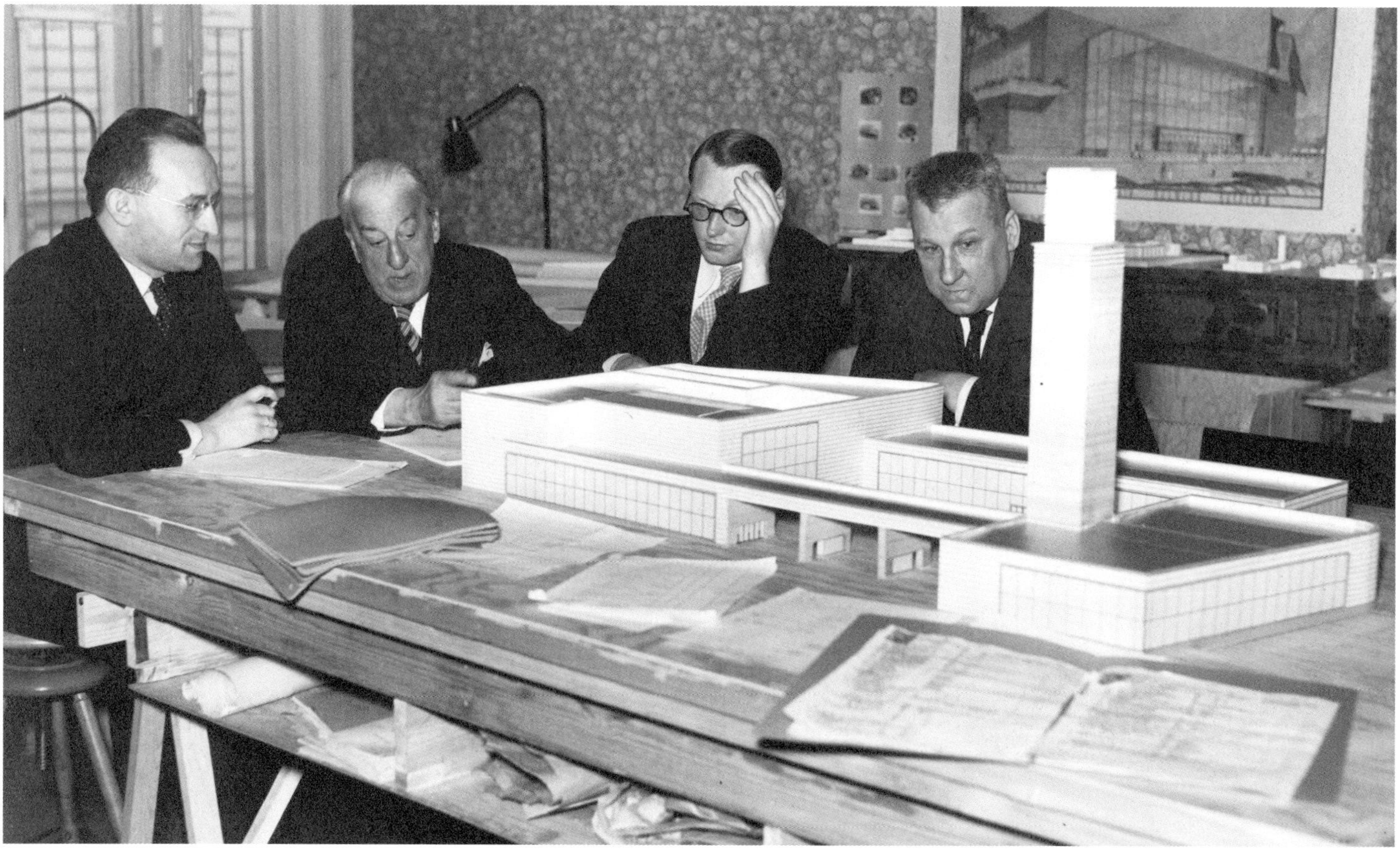

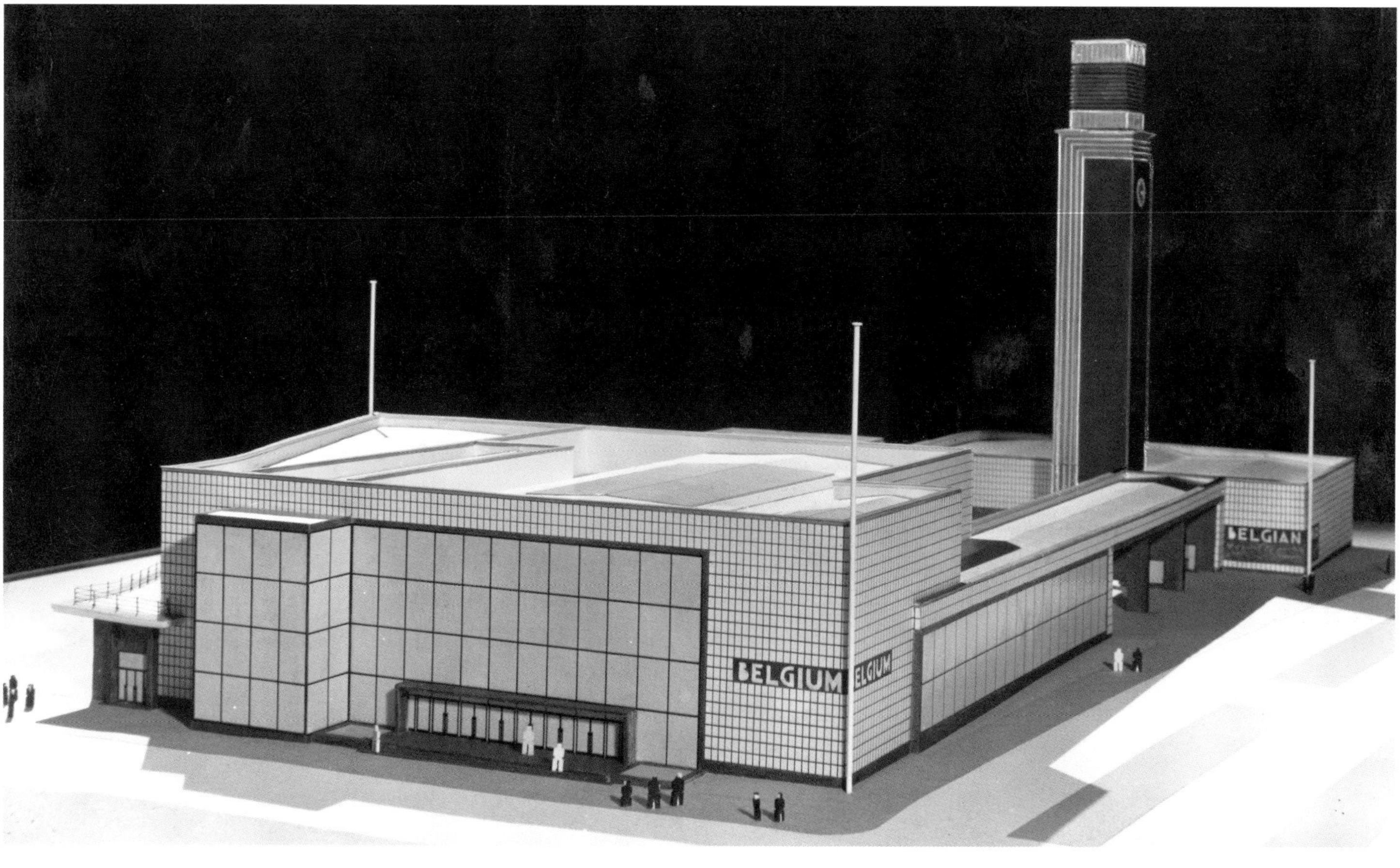
BELGIUM
ELGIUM
BELGIAN

New York World's Fair, Belgian section, 1939

New York World's Fair, Belgian section, 1939

Ostend Casino-Kursaal, 1953

Villa Luft, Kapellen, 1955

Model of the EBES tower, Antwerp, Léon Stynen & Hugo Van Kuyck, 1956

Urban planning study, development plan for Wezenberg, Antwerp, 1962

Model of the Telex building, Brussels, 1959

St Rita's Church, Harelbeke, 1959

Model for the BP Building, Antwerp, 1959

BP Building, Antwerp, 1959

Canteen of the BP Building, Antwerp, 1961

Housing and office complex De Zonnewijzer, office Stynen and De Meyer, Antwerp, 1954

Stynen & De Meyer offices, Antwerp, 1954

Interior train Amsterdam-Paris TEE, 1963

Interior ferry boat Ostend-Dover, 1953

Project for the Antwerp National Contemporary Arts Museum, 1968

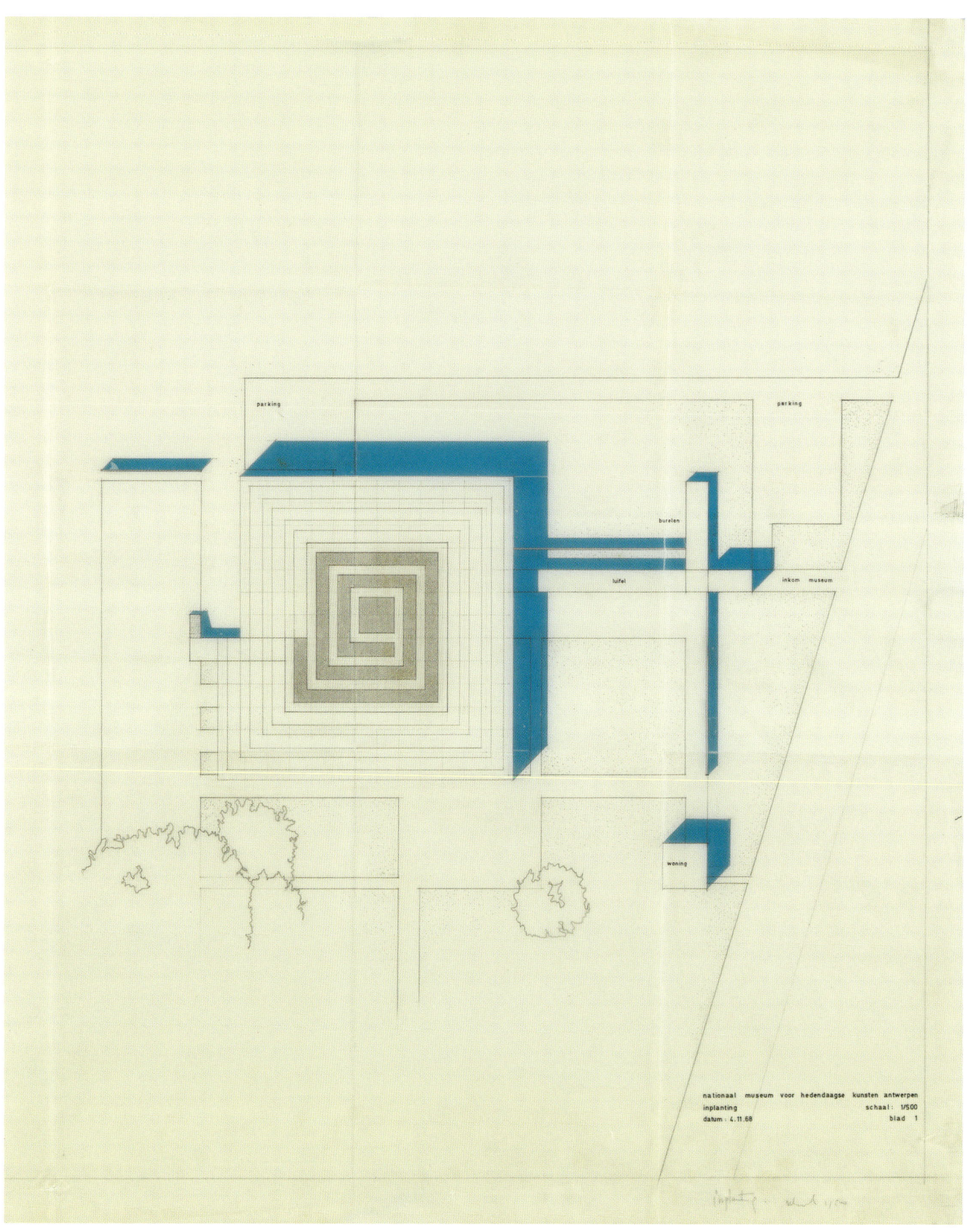

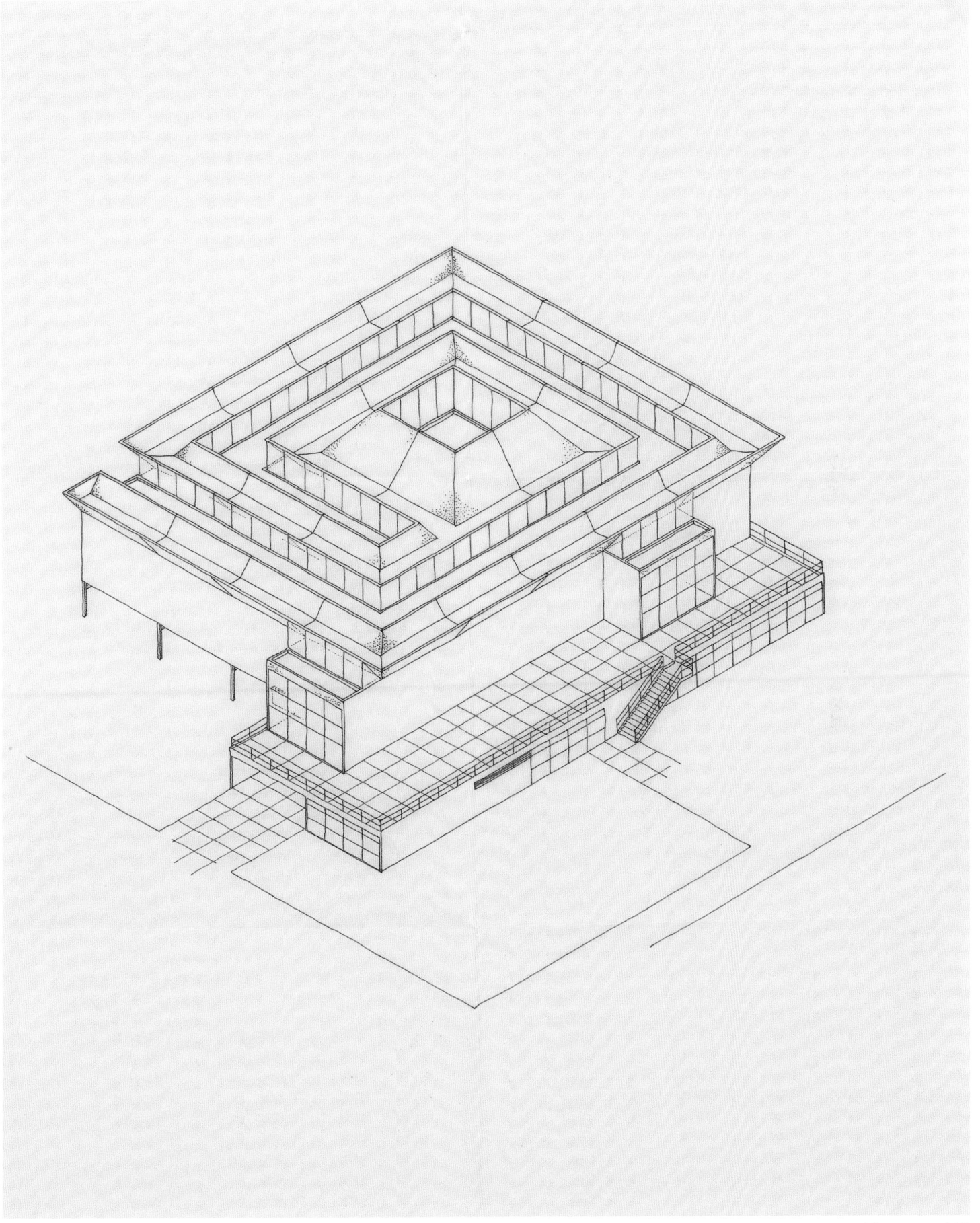
Project for the Antwerp National Contemporary Arts Museum, 1968

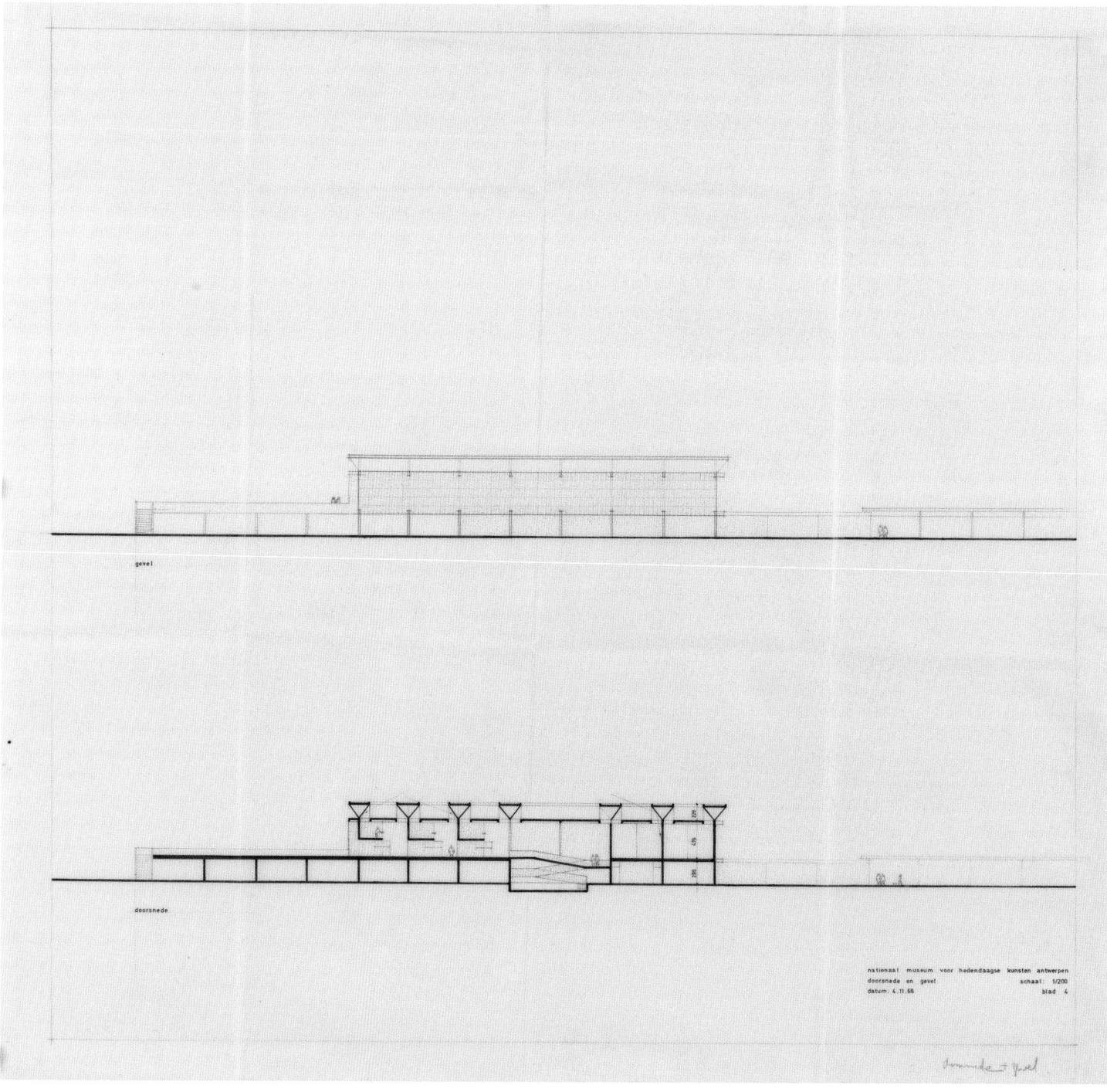

Project for the Antwerp National Contemporary Arts Museum, 1968

The Conservatory, DeSingel, Antwerp, 1962–87

105

LEON STYNEN ARCHITECTE S. R. A. A.

LE RUSTOORD, home de cure

ARCHITECTE LEON STYNEN

Ci-dessus : Le « Rustoord ». Aspect général. Arch. Léon Stynen. L'entreprise anversoise a été assumée par la Sté Ame Entreprises Générales Van Der Straeten Frères, 62, rue de l'Empereur, à Anvers, tél. 210.76.

Conformément à la loi, la « Caisse interprofessionnelle d'Allocations familiales », organisme anversois agréé par arrêté royal, consacre annuellement une part de ses importants bénéfices à des œuvres d'hygiène sociale de caractère familial.
La lutte contre la tuberculose et les maladies infantiles se plaçant au premier rang de son activité philanthropique, la caisse établit au bénéfice de ses assujettis un système prophylactique et curatif comportant : un corps d'infirmières visiteuses, un centre médical d'examen et de diagnostic, plusieurs dispensaires, un magnifique home de cure d'air édifié récemment.
Les institutions de cure d'air de l'agglomération anversoise étant insuffisantes, la caisse agit intelligemment en acquérant le domaine « Hof Ten Bosch », composé de tren-

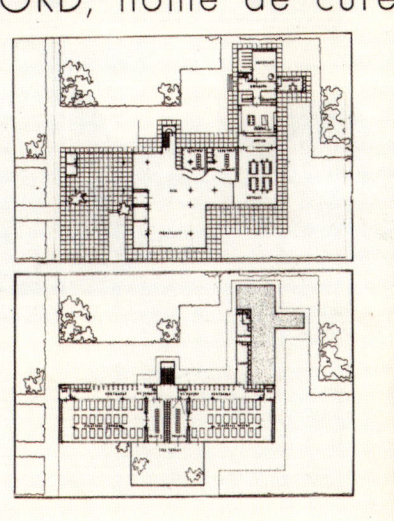

Plans du rez-de-chaussée (ou-dessus) et de l'étage (ci-contre) du « Rustoord ». Architecte Léon Stynen.

d'air pour enfants, à Brasschaet

Un aspect de la façade postérieure, vers l'escalier. Arch. Léon Stynen.
Tous les travaux de peinture ont été effectués par la firme bien connue David Petrie Limited, S. A., rue du Brésil, 27-29, à Anvers, tél. 221.75.
L'installation frigorifique placée dans cet Etablissement comporte un frigo maçonné, mesurant extérieurement 1 m. 80 x 1 m. 30 x 2 m. 20 de hauteur, équipé avec groupe frigorifique automatique Lebrun au chlorure de méthyle, d'une puissance de 1/3 HP.

Vue extérieure vers l'escalier. Arch. Léon Stynen.
Le monte-charge de la buanderie a été construit et installé par la Société Anonyme « Ascenseurs E. Thiry », 35, rue de la Violette, Anvers.
Toutes les installations électriques comprenant la machinerie, l'éclairage et la téléphonie intérieure ont été réalisés par Henri Fredrix, 61, rue Grein, Anvers, tél. 543.86.
Dans cette construction, le tapis en caoutchouc « Gomaflor » Bergougnan a été utilisé, entre autres, pour garnir les marches d'escalier. Compagnie Bergougnan Belge, à Evergem-Rabot, lez-Gand.

te hectares de sapins, d'un grand verger et de plaines de gazon pour y ériger le « Rustoord » sur les plans de l'architecte Stynen. D'une clarté remarquable les plans que nous reproduisons montrent que Léon Stynen domine aisément le problème. Leur simplicité et leur fermeté, leur valeur fonctionnelle s'expriment avec probité et force dans le rythme général et les détails de la bâtisse. Celle-ci est orientée au sud-est. Tous les locaux occupés par les enfants sont disposés de ce côté, lequel possède le meilleur ensoleillement. Seuls les locaux de service sont orientés au nord-est.
Explorons rapidement le « Rustoord » ruisselant de clarté.
Voici au rez-de-chaussée un préau couvert entouré de châssis garnis de glace; devant ces châssis sont placées des balustrades de protection. Cette disposition permet aux enfants de jouer à l'abri des intempéries sans qu'ils soient privés du grand air et de la vue des bois. De grandes terrasses d'une superficie approximative de 300 m2 le précédent.
En passant par le préau on accède au hall, qui constitue une grande salle de jeux, et sur lequel donnent la salle d'attente et le bureau de la direction. Dans le hall sont placés les vestiaires et lavatories séparés par des écrans courbés.
Tous les châssis peuvent glisser les uns derrière les autres de façon à former en cas de besoin une vaste place de jeu composée des terrasses du hall et du préau couvert. La superficie de cet ensemble s'élève à 650 m2.
Le hall tient de réfectoire dont les châssis également coulissants font communiquer cette salle avec les terrasses. Derrière le réfectoire se trouve le quartier des locaux de service comprenant de spacieux offices et cuisines équipés de façon impeccable, une salle destinée au nettoyage des légumes, un économat pourvu de glacières et de silos, une buanderie et un local pour le repassage. A proximité des locaux de service l'architecte a très utilement prévu une salle de repos pour le personnel, avec vestiaire y attenant.
Revenant au grand hall on gagne l'escalier conduisant aux étages; cet escalier étant réalisé à claire-voie ne forme pas un écran opaque. Près de cet escalier sont situées les armoires à jouets.
Deux vastes dortoirs de 35 lits chacun (celui de droite destiné aux filles, celui de gauche aux garçons) constituent l'élément essentiel de l'étage.

Clarté

1939
numéro 7
5 francs
12e année

art et art décoratif
architecture

Un salon du "Baudouinville".

Juillet
1939

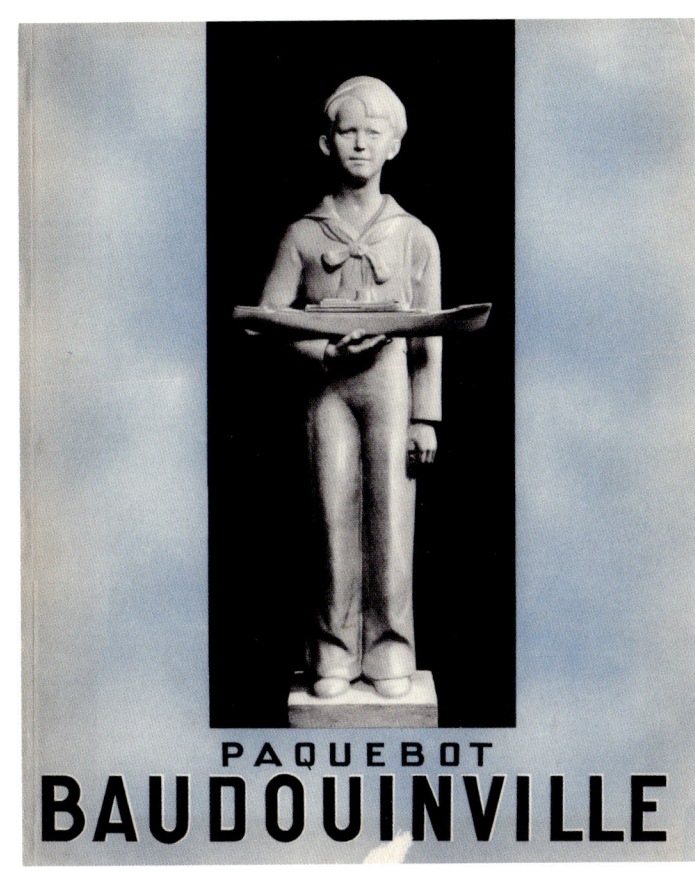

Salle à manger de première classe. Ce local particulièrement vaste dispose d'une hauteur de deux ponts. Il a été traité par l'architecte L. Stynen avec finesse et sobriété. Les tons verts particulièrement doux des tapis et des rideaux s'harmonisent avec les lambris de palissandre d'Afrique. Cette salle peut se transformer en cinéma.

Photos Mayer.

BOUWKUNST en WEDEROPBOUW

MAANDSCHRIFT GEWIJD AAN ARCHITECTUUR · URBANISME
BOUWTECHNIEK · DECORATIEVE KUNST · BINNENHUISKUNST

Inhoud

Wederopbouw en Aesthetica,
    door prof. Henry Van de Velde, algemeen adviseur voor Bouwkunde bij het Commissariaat-Generaal voor 's Lands Wederopbouw.

New York... stad vol verwachting,
    door architect Leo Stynen.

Bouwtechniek : Duurzaamheid en samenstelling van muurmaterialen (vervolg en slot),
    door R. Fitzmaurice, B. Sc.

Boekbesprekingen.

REDACTIE EN BEHEER : 37, Zennestraat, 37, BRUSSEL
Telefoon 12.10.85   Postch. 442.91 (Bouwkroniek)   H. R. Brussel 34666
ABONNEMENTSPRIJZEN :
België : 6 maanden (6 nummers) 28 fr.; 12 maanden (12 nummers) 50 fr.
Buitenland : 12 maanden 60 fr. (12 Belgas)
LOSSE NUMMERS : 5 frank (Buitenland 1,50 Belga)

1ste jaar / N° 9 / September 1941

CASINO A CHAUDFONTAINE.
ARCHITECTE LEON STYNEN.
(PHOTO MALEVEZ)

AOUT 1939 — 81

DANS CE NUMERO :
PLAINES DE JEUX,
PARCS D'ENFANTS,
PLAGES, CASINO,
VILLAS, ETC.

BATIR

4 FR. LE NUMÉRO • REVUE MENSUELLE ILLUSTRÉE
D'ARCHITECTURE, D'ART ET DE DÉCORATION

Le Casino de Chaudfontaine. Vue du grand hall. Au fond, l'entrée du dancing, sous une peinture murale de Van Vlasselaer. A l'extrémité droite, l'entrée vers le salon particulier. Architecte Léon Stynen.
Les somptueuses tentures du Casino, ainsi que les tapis, linoléums, tissus de sièges et fenêtres du Palace, proviennent des Etablissements Fernand Van de Ven, S. A., Bruxelles, le collaborateur de la décoration intérieure.
Les luminaires du hall dessinés par l'architecte Stynen, les lampadaires de la salle de danse et les plafonniers des chambres à coucher du Palace ont été exécutés et placés par Eug. Bouchier, fabricant d'appareils d'éclairage, successeur de « Demblon », 39, rue Quellin, Anvers.

Ci-dessous : le grand hall. Le coin de lecture et de correspondance. Dans la paroi courbe, un remarquable motif décoratif de Van Vlasselaer. Architecte Léon Stynen.
Mobilier exécuté par les Ateliers d'Art De Coene Frères, à Courtrai.
Tous les travaux de peinture, tant intérieurs qu'extérieurs, ont été effectués par : Peinture De Rooy, S. P. R. L., Décorations et peintures, rue Général Drubbel, 52, Berchem-Anvers.

calme et harmonieux, le bâtiment est ouvert au soleil sur toutes ses faces.
Son parti constructif comporte une ossature en béton armé, un remplissage en briques, un parement principal en dalles de schiste ardoisier encadré de briques blanches de Ligne. Les châssis métalliques, les bras d'acier portant l'auvent, les boiseries et les enseignes sont peints en blanc.
Les quatre façades, très différentes, accusent les fonctions si diverses des locaux qu'elles abritent.
Vers la Vesdre, le grand hall montre une baie monumentale profilée en onde. Vers le chemin de fer, le retour de la façade principale s'interrompt devant la porte privée du directeur, encadrée d'oculis carrés chargés d'éclairer le corridor. De ce côté du bâtiment des cuisines, très sobre, montre une façade unie en briques blanches garnie de nombreux petits châssis basculants qui assurent aux locaux de travail une circulation d'air excellente.
La façade postérieure, celle du dancing, n'est qu'une baie vitrée, dont la partie inférieure ouvrante assure une communication généreuse avec la terrasse du tea room. Cette terrasse, très spacieuse, est couverte d'un store rigide de nuance orange, tendu sur un bâti en tubes d'acier. Au pied de la terrasse se déploie une belle pelouse. Plus tard, une piscine d'agrément sera créée dans son axe.
L'entrée sous auvent, la longue baie en loggia, le généreux parement en ardoise et une délicate garniture florale donnent du caractère à la façade principale.
Le petit hall d'entrée, d'un bleu lumineux est décoré d'un léger semis d'étoiles. Le hall principal donne sur une grande impression de fraîcheur. Il assure l'accès, à droite, du bureau de la direction, au secrétariat, au salon des jeux et, au fond, au dancing-restaurant, au vestiaire et locaux sanitaires.
Le grand hall est meublé en merisier et tissus de ton

L'entrée du dancing, surmontée d'un beau motif de Van Vlasselaer. A droite : la grande volve publicitaire abritant les entrées du vestiaire et des lavatories. Architecte Léon Stynen.
(Photos Malevez.)

344

Le hall. Vue vers l'entrée du salon particulier. Motifs décoratifs de Van Vlasselaer.
Tapis exécutés par Al. et Ed. David, rue Longue, 55, Ostende.

façade et par des lanterneaux étroits garnis de dalles de verres. Les baies sont dotées de châssis coulissants. Les lanterneaux abritent des diffuseurs électriques.
Sur l'enduit général granuleux, de ton beige, les grands motifs décoratifs de Van Vlasselaer formant frise prennent une grande allure. On ne sait s'il faut préférer la solidité des compositions, l'élégance du dessin, le charme des combinaisons de nuances. L'ensemble révèle un esprit très poétique et une connaissance parfaite des ressources de la décoration murale en tons plats.
Les ameublements du restaurant et du bar sont en chêne cérusé et gris tissus accordés. Les proportions horizontales du comptoir et du buffet du bar, ses parois roses, son plafond ondulé, ses gorges éclairantes dissimulées composent un coin charmant. L'écran courbe séparant le bar de l'entrée des croupiers et du bureau du changeur est orné d'une composition de Van Vlasselaer d'un style néocubiste remarquable.
Le dancing, de forme trapézoïdale, est également décoré d'une frise de Van Vlasselaer. Sur deux mètres de hauteur et 72 mètres de longueur, c'est une suite de motifs ornementaux d'une imagination parfois gratuite, toujours spirituelle, parfai-

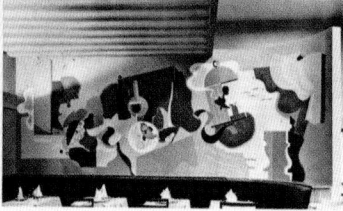

Le restaurant que prolonge le salon particulier. Les peintures sont de Van Vlasselaer. Architecte Léon Stynen.
Tapis dessiné par l'architecte et exécuté par Al. et Ed. David, 55, rue Longue, à Ostende.

soufre pour les sièges, orangé pour les rideaux. Le tapis vert bleuâtre est parsemé d'étoiles blanches et brunes. Sur les parois d'un blanc mat de coquille d'œuf règnent des peintures de Van Vlasselaer exécutées en tons plats. De puissants diffuseurs en acier fournissent un éclairage indirect.
Le salon mesure 35 mètres sur 18 mètres. Une superficie de 130 m2 a été réservée au bar-restaurant. La salle est éclairée par la baie longue et basse qui forme loggia en

Une intéressante composition décorative de Van Vlasselaer occupant la face interne de l'écran qui sépare le bar-restaurant du salon particulier. Architecte Léon Stynen.
(Photos Malevez.)

345

revue
mensuelle
d'architecture
de
décoration
et d'art ménager

18e année
Février 1962
Prix : 30 frs
Editions
Art et
Technique
Bruxelles

la maison 2

studio architetti BBPR · via dei Chiostri 2 · 14220 · Milano

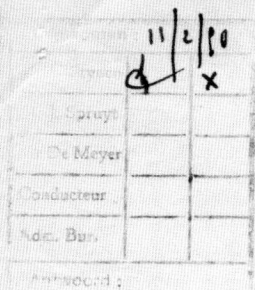

dr. arch. Lodovico B. Belgiojoso
dr. arch. Enrico Peressutti
dr. arch. Ernesto N. Rogers

Milan, le 6 fevrier 1950

Mon cher Stynen,
merci pour votre aimable lettre du 31 janvier.
Je crains que je n'ai pas beaucoup des choses à vous racconter au sujet de notre Commission.

Je peux vous dire qu'étant à Londre pendant deux mois à l'Architectural Association School of Architecture (34-36 Bedford Square - London W. C. 1), j'ai partecipé à la Commission du groupe anglais qui à été faite dans ce temps; le président de celle-ci est Mr. Robert Jordan, directeur de l'Ecole même.

Je crois qu'il est trés utile si vous lui écrivez pour établir les contacts.

De ma part je ferai de mon mieux pour tirer tous les filets.

Ici nous avons aussi établi dans le groupe du CIAM italien une Commission pour l'Education dont je m'occupe personnellement.

Dans le domain general du CIAM, Mr. Gropius est le président et moi même le vice-présidant.
Pour le moment c'est tout.

Les anglais ont des bonnes intentions pour faire aussi cette année une Summer School.

Veuillez m'écrire, s'il vous plait, vos décision aprés le réunion dont vous me parlez.

Croyez, mon cher Stynen, à ma meilleure amitié.

Ernesto N. Rogers.

Anvers, le 15 avril 1950

LS/CV

Monsieur Rogers,
Studio Architetti BBPR,
Via dei Chiostri, 2
MILANO.

Mon cher Rogers,

Merci mille fois pour votre lettre du 6 du mois dernier.
Le groupe belge s'est réuni et m'a chargé de conduire les travaux de la commission pour l'enseignement.
Nous ferons une enquête sur les methodes d'enseignement dans notre pays. Nous sommes bien documenté pour ce qui concerne l'enseignement officiel, mais nous le sommes moins pour l'enseignement libre.
Je vous tiendrai au courant de nos travaux et j'espère que de votre côté, vous me tiendrez au courant des travaux du groupe italien.
S'avez vous qui s'occupe de la question dans les autres pays ?
Recevez, mon cher Rogers, mes bonnes amitiés et croyez moi votre,

A Henry Van de Velde Oberägeri - Suisse.

Bruxelles, le 5/12/1952.

Souvent j'ai eu l'intention de vous écrire, mon cher ami Van de Velde, mais chaque fois je m'en suis abstenu, avec raison je pense. C'est que "La Cambre" était bien malade et je ne voulais pas, je ne pouvais pas vous mentir ou vous inquieter.
Vous ne serez pas étonné d'apprendre que plusieurs professeurs ne semblaient plus se souvenir des raisons pour lesquelles l'Institut fut créé. L'esprit d'équipe aussi avait disparu et chacun s'était retiré dans sa tanière, c'est le cas de le dire, pour agir plus commodément, ou pire, pour ne plus agir du tout. Il a fallu redresser cela petit à petit, répèter à ces inamovibles professeurs ce qu'est leur mission ; plus souvent encore leur rappeler cette vérité fondamentale "La fonction crée la forme" principe fondamental du message que vous nous avez laissé. Il a fallu aussi faire appel au courage sinon à la conscience professionnelle laquelle semble bien avoir foutu le camp. Certains se sont ressaisis, mais il faudra beaucoup de patience et pas mal de persévérance pour rétablir les choses.

Jamais la séparation de l'Art et de l'Industrie n'a été aussi prononcée, jamais n'avons nous été aussi éloignés des recherches vers la coordination architecturale dont on parle tant et pour laquelle on fait si peu.
Je crois cependant que nous ne sortirons de l'impasse dans laquelle nous nous trouvons que lorsque les hommes témoigneront du désir commun de vivre mieux dans une plus grande beauté d'esprit et de coeur.

Une chose est réconfortante, c'est le sérieux avec lequel, enfin! les élèves considèrent les études qu'ils poursuivent chez nous ; l'esprit d'invention ne leur manque pas et ils comprennent qu'à "La Cambre" il est permis de regarder librement l'Univers, de le penser librement, de l'exprimer librement suivant sa conscience, son intelligence et son tempérament.
J'ai obtenu des professeurs aussi qu'ils cultivent le doute en ce qu'il a de constructif, ce doute qui fait que l'élève reste toujours persuadé que ce qu'il fait pourrait être mieux.

./..

Allocution prononcée à Zug à l'occasion du nonantième anniversaire

d'Henry Van de Velde.

 Il n'est pas indispensable, ~~je pense~~, de faire de longs discours pour dire combien nous sommes heureux ~~et fiers à la fois~~ de nous trouver autour de vous, ~~aujourd'hui, mon~~ cher maître et ami ~~~~, Henry Van de Velde, pour fêter votre nonantième anniversaire.

 Vous êtes né en Belgique, à Anvers, plus exactement sur les bords d'~~un fleuve magnifique~~ "l'Escaut" que ~~vous aimez bien, mais~~ que le destin vous fit quitter dès votre jeunesse, pour aller accomplir par ce ~~vaste~~ monde une ~~plus grande~~ mission ~~d'esthéticien et d'architecte~~; cette mission vous l'avez portée très vite et très haut sur le plan international et à 25 ans, déjà vous étiez un grand Monsieur.

 D'autres que moi, peut être, diront aujourd'hui encore ce que représente votre oeuvre et sa valeur dans la recherche de l'esprit et de la pureté des formes; qu'il me soit permis toutefois de rester exclusivement sur le terrain de l'amitié et de vous parler très simplement d'une chose simple, mais dont le monde actuel qu'il soit artistique, politique ou autre ne semble plus avoir aucune notion; c'est de la droiture des intentions et de l'honnêteté des arguments que l'on peut faire valoir dans la défense d'une opinion.

 Or c'est à votre droiture d'esprit, à l'honnêteté de l'argumentation philosophique qui traverse toute votre oeuvre écrite comme elle s'exprime aussi dans votre oeuvre bâtie, c'est à cette beauté d'esprit, à votre intelligence, à la sûreté de votre jugement, à la générosité de vos actes, à la discipline et au sacrifice de votre vie que j'apporte au nom de tous vos amis l'hommage le plus respectueux, le plus ému et aussi le plus affectueux, et en particulier l'hommage de vos amis de Belgique et très spécialement de tous ceux, qui, comme J.Minne ici présent, travaillent dans la lumière de l'Institut de la Cambre que vous avez créé il y a 25 ans.

 Responsable de la destinée de votre Ecole, de cette maison de culture vivante, de ce haut lieu de liberté spirituelle, je vous fais la promesse de travailler dans le même esprit de vérité et de modestie dont vous nous avez donné le magnifique exemple et dont nous ne cesserons de nous inspirer toujours.

 Merci de tout coeur, mon cher ami, et n'oubliez jamais je vous prie que nous vous aimons intensément comme vous nous aimez.

            Léon Stynen,
            Directeur de l'Institut de la Cambre.

      Le 3 Avril, 1953.

LE CORBUSIER   Paris, le 29 Mars 1954

Monsieur Léon STIJNEN
Abbaye de la Cambre, 21
BRUXELLES

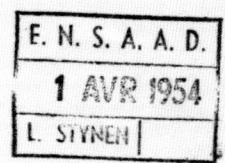

Mon cher Stijnen,

    Retour des Indes, j'ai pris connaissance d'une note de Wogenscky du 12 février 54 me mettant au courant de votre projet relatif à l'Exposition de Bruxelles en 1958 : réalisation d'un musée en spirale carrée.

    Je vous remercie d'avoir pensé à moi et j'accepte volontiers votre proposition car j'ai étudié ce problème depuis 1930. Il a un jour pris le nom de "Musée de la Connaissance", ce qui représente un point de vue muséographique tout à fait nouveau et capable d'être socialement utile. J'ai à plusieurs reprises inséré cette idée dans mes projets et il a fallu l'aventure des Indes pour que réalisation s'en suive. Actuellement à Ahmedabad, le "Musée de la Connaissance" est en pleine construction au coeur du Centre Civique de cette ville d'un million d'habitants. Autour du Musée lui-même viennent se grouper divers corollaires destinés à former un tout.

    Concernant Bruxelles, il s'agit d'un outil entièrement neuf d'exposition d'objets et d'idées, permettant une mobilité totale dans la plus grande facilité.

    Il faudrait que nous puissions en parler de vive-voix afin que dans vos projets il vous soit possible de prévoir l'emplacement utile. En effet la nature du terrain et sa contenance sont déterminantes. Avez-vous l'occasion de venir prochainement à Paris ? Personnellement je suis immobilisé ici par des devoirs impératifs.

    Je serai heureux de lire votre réponse, et vous prie de croire, mon cher Stijnen, à mes sentiments les meilleurs.

35, RUE DE SÈVRES - PARIS (6e)
TÉL. : LITTRÉ 99-62

LE CORBUSIER

5

LE CORBUSIER

Paris, le 12 Juin 1959

Monsieur Léon J. STYNEN
85, Avenue de la Colonie
A N V E R S
Belgique

Mon cher Stynen,

Ma vie se passe de voyage en voyage !

Merci de votre agissante sympathie. Voici le mot d'explication réclamé :

Un navire est fait d'une coque, d'une mécanique, d'une hôtellerie (insignifiante ou très importante).

Les trois choses sont, chacune, l'oeuvre d'un spécialiste).

Les navires à traction mécanique ont longtemps été des ensembles hybrides :

- aérodynamique
- vie à l'intérieur
- coordination volumétrique des choses
- en un mot, harmonie.

Les bateaux de toutes les époques ont été superbes chaque fois. Il est aujourd'hui possible d'apporter l'harmonie dans un ensemble moderne; c'est cela qui m'intéresse. Il ne s'agit pas une minute de proposer une décoration ou des vestiges d'architecture terrestre. Encore une fois, il s'agit d'harmonie.

Voilà, mon cher Stynen.

J'espère que tout va bien pour vous et je vous salue bien amicalement.

Le Corbusier

LE CORBUSIER

35, RUE DE SÈVRES : PARIS (6°)
TÉL. : LITTRÉ 99-62

LEON M.J.R. STYNEN   Bruxelles 3/12/65.

Mon cher Lecorbusier

"Chandigarh". Ce n'est pas sans regrets que j'ai quitté ce chantier, où malgré les très médiocres choses qui s'y accomplissent s'achève une grande œuvre, la vôtre, "Le Capitole".

Que vous dire, mon cher Lecorbusier, sinon que votre architecture, semblable à celles d'un lointain passé, est empreinte du soleil.
Vous féliciter serait banal, mais veuillez accepter, très cher Lecorbusier, ces quelques essais photographiques en modeste et très amical hommage.

                                    Votre
                                    L. Stynen

Inutile de vous dire que les films vous appartiennent.

qui, bien au delà de la simple raison d'être les crée toutes — rendant possible le dialogue entre l'homme qui la contemple et la conscience qui l'habite.

LE CORBUSIER   Paris, le 5 Décembre 1963

Monsieur Léon STYNEN
Architecte
Abbaye de la Cambre
B R U X E L L E S

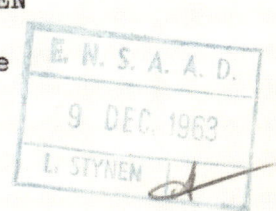

Mon cher Stynen,

M. Bekkers, de Bruxelles, est venu hier m'apporter une grande série de photographies faites par vous à Chandigarh. C'est un très beau cadeau et je vous en remercie vivement.

C'est la première fois que je reçois une information sur Chandigarh. Depuis dix années je demande des documents et je n'en ai jamais obtenus. Les vôtres sont faits par un architecte qui sait voir.

Ce que m'a remis M. Bekkers concerne très particulièrement le Secrétariat et des extérieurs du Capitol. Il y a très peu de choses de la Haute-Cour qui est un très bon bâtiment.

Vous avez su prendre vos documents en plein paysage et c'est très éloquent. La seule observation qui est à faire c'est qu'à "Chandigarh Ville" les maisons sont dans le gazon tandis qu'à "Chandigarh Capitol" il n'y a que de la brousse (du sable et des mauvaises herbes).

Ma participation à Chandigarh a été limitée (non pas par ma volonté) :

    a/ au tracé général de la ville (urbanisation)
    b/ création du "Secteur", des "V 3" et des "V 4", mise en application de la "Règle des 7 V"
    c/ au tracé du Capitol et construction des palais du Capitol
    d/ des velléités d'organisation du "Centre Civique"

Merci encore de vos photos et cordialement à vous.

LE CORBUSIER

35, RUE DE SÈVRES - PARIS 6e
TÉL : LITTRÉ 99-62

HIS CONTEMPORARIES

MARC DUBOIS

Léon Stynen in an international context

The major retrospective exhibition *Léon Stynen. A Life of Architecture 1899–1990*, organized in 2018 at deSingel by the VAi/Flemish Architecture Institute, brought to public attention the impressive oeuvre of one of the most fascinating Belgian architects of the twentieth century. This oeuvre represents half a century of Belgian architecture, from Stynen's graduation in 1922 through to 1977, the year in which he ended his professional career. It has not, however, received the international exposure it deserves and indeed is still not fully appreciated in Belgium. As in 2018, this publication seeks to place an exceptional oeuvre within an international panorama.[1]

Many factors that guide a person's life can bring about unexpected turns: family background and upbringing, primary and higher education, social background, personal experiences, influences and stimuli. The economic conditions of the time and a host of chance events and encounters can also direct a person's course in life. And there is also the intelligence to seize unexpected opportunities, which ultimately become important links in a career and a body of work.

The biography of an artist gauges the multitude of contacts and influences in order to grasp its subject's life and oeuvre. This applies equally to architects, who also draw creative direction from the work of other architects and from publications. Dividing an oeuvre into phases usually revolves around pivotal moments in a person's life. This certainly applies to Léon Stynen (1899–1990). Without discussing all his projects, this text seeks to emphasize Stynen's assimilative capacity, and to examine how his work expresses his sensitivity to the era in which it was created. Stynen's oeuvre is more than the sum of his buildings; it is the path he travelled, a path in which relationships also arise between the various creations. An architect does not work in a void and what he comes up with always has affinities with examples from the distant past or present day. An interest in new materials and their applications can also radically determine an oeuvre.

There are architects who have written a lot, while their architectural legacy has remained rather limited. For Stynen, the ambition to build always prevailed over committing to paper literary and social reflections. He developed an exceptionally wide personal network, as is evident from the variety of his clients. Industrialists from the port, and the diamond and fashion sectors all gave him commissions. Private individuals and government agencies placed their confidence in him, enabling him to produce important buildings that are now part of Belgium's modern heritage. On his own initiative he also launched proposals like a museum in the Middelheim Park or along the Antwerp quays – projects that eventually disappeared into archive boxes.

Stynen was a socialist, but not one with hard, militant convictions. A true aristocrat, he had the gift of being diplomatic, but at the same time the courage to distance himself when he did not believe in bringing together a diversity of architects around a particular project. For example, after fierce discussions, he quit the team commissioned to construct the new National Administrative Centre in Brussels.

Stynen had a great sense of professionalism and defended the importance of the designer's role in creating a built environment. He attached great value to a knowledge of construction engineering in order to deliver good buildings. He assimilated the modernist formal language, but on a constructive level he took far fewer structural risks than avant-garde architects like Huib Hoste (1881–1957), Victor Bourgeois (1897–1962) or Gaston Eysselinck (1907–1953). For Stynen, architecture was the art of building, as it was also for Louis Herman De Koninck (1896–1984).

One generation succeeds another, but sometimes they also overlap. Around 1930, the second generation of modernist architects came to the fore. The first and difficult battle for modern architecture had already been fought by figures such as Hoste, Bourgeois and De Koninck. In addition to Léon Stynen, Gaston Eysselinck, Renaat Braem (1910–2001), Walter Van den Broeck (1905–1945) and Julien Schillemans (1906–1943) were other emerging talents in Flanders. Young architects like Stanislas Jasinski (1901–1978) and Paul-Amaury Michel (1912–1988) also emerged in Brussels, and in Wallonia architects Emile Parent (1910–1985), Albert Tibaux (1908–1985), Edward Klutz (1909–1987), Paul Fitchy (1908–1993) and Yvon Falise (1908–1981) formed Groupe L'Équerre in 1935.

Architects look up to the great master builders of their day. This was certainly the case for the architects of L'Équerre in Liège, who invited Le Corbusier (1887–1965) himself to participate in the basic plan for the *Exposition internationale de l'Eau* in 1939, which however ended in disappointment. Stynen also had great respect for Le Corbusier, but also for the work of other internationally renowned architects. This was reflected in a number of his projects, which is why we place his oeuvre in a broader, more international context.

Classical architecture as a foundation
Stynen received his training at the Royal Academy of Fine Arts in Antwerp between 1915 and 1922. His teachers were renowned master builders, who gave the port city its architectural glory. They were trained in the great tradition of the beaux-arts, which entailed a vision of the craft. The well-structured training at the Academy aimed to pass on the noble craft of architectural composition. In this connection, the theories of Marcus Vitruvius Pollio (1st century BC), a Roman soldier, architect and engineer, and his book *De architectura libri decem* were decisive. Vitruvius' three basic principles of good architecture were *firmitas* (firmness), *utility* (user-friendliness) and *venustas* (beauty). That trinity was also important to Stynen.
A building had to be built soundly with knowledge of the materials. It had to be functional, with the service factor for the user essential. Finally, an architect had to strive for beauty, fundamentally determined by the search for the right proportions, such as the golden ratio, which divides up a façade composition in such a way that the ratio of the smallest to the largest part is the same as that of the largest part to the whole. After 1945, Stynen used the *modulor* measurement system developed by Le Corbusier. Stynen applied this system of proportion, based on the human body, in all his projects, including his interiors.

Architects often conceal their first projects as being no longer relevant in a rapidly changing era. However, the start of an oeuvre remains interesting because it reveals how an architect will position himself and process a multitude of architectural stimuli.

Cover of the exhibition catalogue of *Le Corbusier*, Berlin, 1957, with a representation of his *modulor*

This evolution is fascinating and shows a determination not to simply copy, but to assimilate influences. The process of transforming what already exists can be seen in Stynen's first projects between 1922 and 1930 – in what can be regarded as his development stage. As with other architects, the influences in the 1920s were very diverse, with an emphasis on Dutch and German architectural styles and a growing interest in French Art Deco.

The 1920s

The first major international exhibition after 1918 was the *Exposition internationale des Arts décoratifs et industriels modernes* in Paris in 1925. Stynen visited this exhibition together with his friend, artist René Guiette (1893–1976), whose work he would later integrate into his own home and into the deSingel complex. In Paris, the emphasis was on the formal language of Art Deco, which caused a furore that extended beyond France. There were also innovations that were immediately picked up by the younger generation, such as the pavilion designed by Robert Mallet-Stevens (1886–1945) and the Russian pavilion by Konstantin Melnikov (1890–1974). Le Corbusier's Pavillon de l'Esprit nouveau must have made a great impression on the 26-year-old Stynen and Guiette. The magazine *L'Esprit nouveau*, founded in 1920 by Le Corbusier, and his 1923 book *Vers une architecture* were already widely read in European avant-garde circles. After Paris, Guiette asked Le Corbusier to design a house with studio for him in Antwerp. The Maison Guiette, finished in 1926, was a semi-detached house in which Le Corbusier developed his theoretical Citrohan housing type, as well as his colour palette to achieve the spatial experience in the interior. Undoubtedly, Stynen's visit to Paris in 1925 was the beginning of a lifelong admiration for this Franco-Swiss master builder. The Maison Guiette was included in 1929 in the first part of *Le Corbusier. Œuvre complète, 1910–29*.

Le Corbusier's 1923 book *Vers une architecture* was a bestseller and immediately sold out, as did the second edition from 1924. Perhaps that is why Stynen bought the second edition (1926) of the German version, *Kommende Baukunst*.[2] This German edition also includes two photographs of the Pavillon de l'Esprit nouveau, which Stynen had seen in Paris the year before.

In the 1920s, Antwerp had a dynamic art scene. In 1922, Jozef Peeters (1895–1960) used the term 'community art' to express the bond between art and society. He invited Theo van Doesburg (1883–1931) in early 1920 to give a lecture entitled 'Classical-Baroque-Modern', the text of which was subsequently published in a booklet published by the Antwerp publishing house De Sikkel.[3] The magazines *Het overzicht* (1921–25), founded by Fernand Berckelaers (alias Michel Seuphor, 1901–1999) and Geert Pijnenburg (1896–1980), and *De driehoek* (1925–26) reflect the artistic and social spirit of the times and the international ambitions then at play in Antwerp. Artists and writers like Paul van Ostaijen (1896–1928), Floris (1889–1965) and Oscar Jespers (1887–1970), Paul Joostens (1889–1960), Jozef Peeters, Georges Vantongerloo (1886–1965) and Jos Léonard (1892–1957) contributed to a dynamic art scene in the city on the Scheldt.[4]

In the years after the First World War, many architects were commissioned, along with sculptors, to design monuments commemorating the war victims. Stynen conceived a monument in Knokke (1921–23), whose plinth clearly consists of a composition of volumes with affinities to the works of another Antwerp artist, Georges Vantongerloo, who had joined De Stijl in the Netherlands.

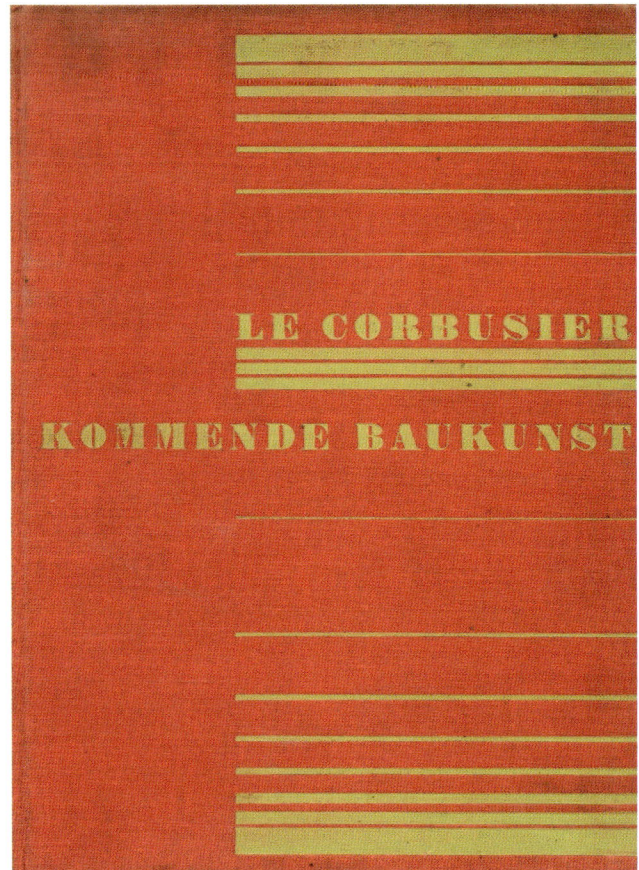

Cover and page of the German edition of Le Corbusier's book *Vers une architecture*, 1923

Stynen saw this assignment as an exercise in developing a new formal language. Like the celebrated Austrian architect Adolf Loos (1870–1933), Stynen regarded a commemorative monument as a full-fledged assignment with which he could make his name as a designer. However, his great ambition to build was prominent from the start of his career. His frame of reference included not only Le Corbusier's work, but also what was being built in the Netherlands and Germany.

The first project with which Stynen consciously moved into the public eye was the Verstrepen house in Boom (1927–28). The building is composed of several very closed blocks, the highest of which consists of the imposing stairwell. The resulting tight plasticity has an affinity with examples from the Netherlands, but also with the sculptural work of Georges Vantongerloo. Stynen later idealized the location, and in photos of the house removed the buildings to the left, creating the impression that this is a detached building surrounded by greenery. To emphasize the modernity of the house, he had it photographed with his own car, a convertible, in the front. Stynen had seen this combination of building and car in publications by Le Corbusier and by German architects. Stynen understood that photography was becoming an increasingly important means of promoting his work. Photographs also exist without this correction, as in *Le Document* (No. 10, 1934). The same house also features in the magazine *Bâtir*, in 1933, with a photo with Stynen's car in the front.[5] Below it is a photo of the Peeters house in Deurne by architect Gaston Eysselinck from 1932. Perhaps rather coincidentally placed together, they are two buildings separated by five years. Stynen's house has a brick composition versus that of the young Eysselinck, who opted for a fragile plaster cladding on the façade, which

Verstrepen house and Peeters house in *Bâtir*, No. 8, 1933

Verstrepen house in *Le Document*, No. 10, 1934

Peeters private residence, architect Gaston Eysselinck, Deurne, 1932

quickly caused problems. Stynen never took such risks and it must have been a disappointment for him to see the stucco walls of Le Corbusier's house for Guiette deteriorating structurally. Perhaps this observation gave Stynen the insight to devote considerable attention to constructive logic, apart from any dogmatic thinking about modern architecture.

In 1928, he entered the competition to design the governor-general's residence in Léopoldville in the Belgian Congo (now Kinshasa), one of Stynen's many unexecuted projects. In this context, Albert Bontridder has pointed to the influence of Frank Lloyd Wright (1867–1959) and the Dutch neo-plasticism of De Stijl.[6] The high tower and the asymmetrical composition in fact refer more to the Hilversum City Hall by architect Willem Marinus Dudok (1884–1974), then under construction, and whose design was already extensively documented in 1924 in the Dutch magazine *Wendingen*. Many architects travelled on study trips to Hilversum, where municipal architect Dudok had drawn up the urbanization plan and built several schools. A visit to Hilversum was the ultimate study trip, the city almost a place of pilgrimage for architects. Another Dutch architect with great resonance was Hendricus Theodorus Wijdeveld (1885–1987), the editor-in-chief of *Wendingen*, a magazine that circulated widely in Flanders. Wijdeveld's ideas on establishing an international working community for architects took more concrete form with an (unexecuted) design for the construction of a centre for that working community in Loosdrecht (1927–28). That project, too, was also published and Stynen's proposal for Léopoldville has a great affinity with it, with a pronounced combination of vertical and horizontal.

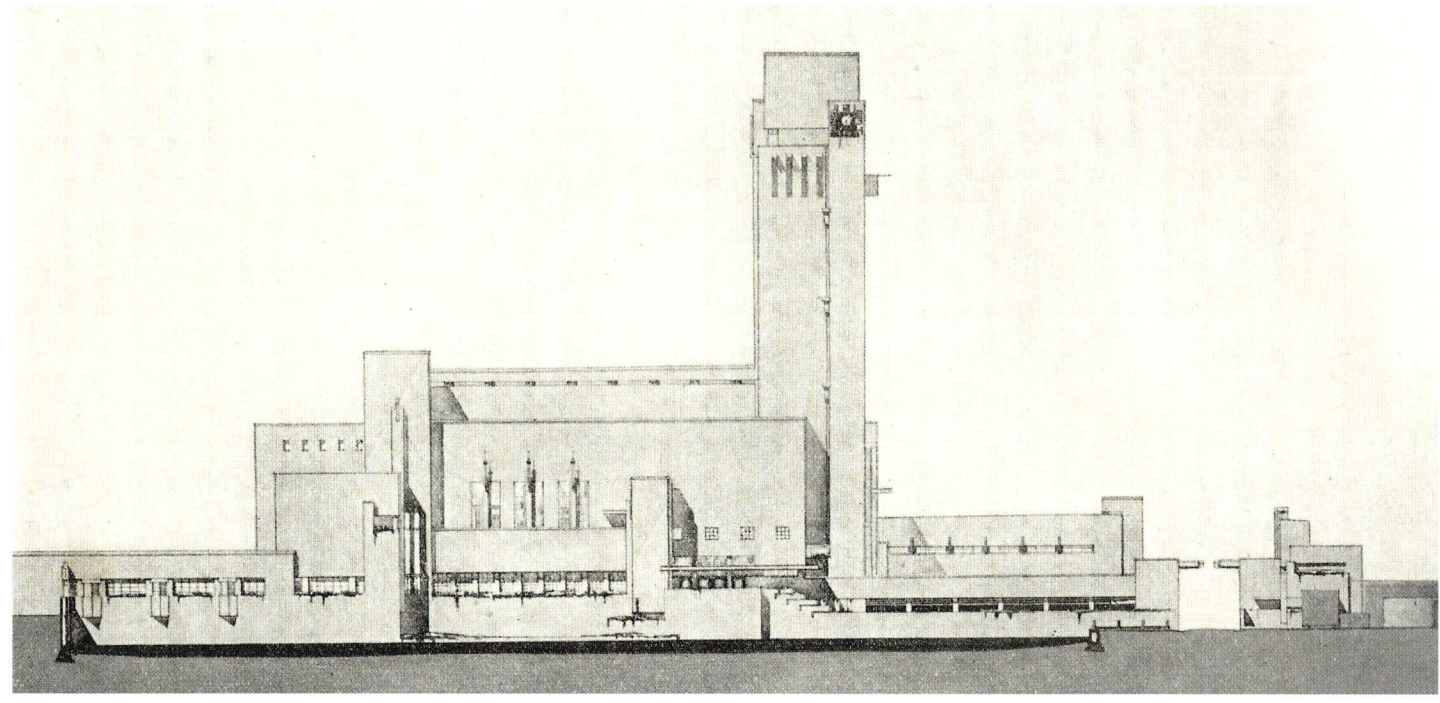

Project for City Hall, Hilversum, architect Willem Marinus Dudok, 1924

The Bauhaus in Weimar, Germany, and then in Dessau represented an innovation in architectural education. Henry van de Velde (1863–1957) was at the forefront of it, even before 1914. In Belgium's progressive architectural environment, people were keen to give him an opportunity to further propagate his educational vision. In 1927, he was able to start a new art school in Brussels, the Institut supérieur des Arts décoratifs or National Higher School for Decorative Arts, now better known as the École de La Cambre. As its director, he put together a team that included Victor Bourgeois and Huib Hoste. From the academic year 1927–28, the first students began at the 'Belgian Bauhaus'. Léon Stynen was director there from 1950 to 1965, succeeding Van de Velde and Herman Teirlinck (1879–1967).[7]

Antwerp 1930
In the run-up to the centenary of Belgian independence in 1930, the cities of Liège and Antwerp were selected in 1926 for a major international exhibition. In Antwerp, the theme was 'Colonies, Maritime and Flemish Art'. Antwerp wanted to profile itself as the modern metropolis on the River Scheldt. The city received a hypermodern airport in Deurne, designed by the Brussels architect Stanislas Jasinski. The most prestigious project was Europe's tallest residential tower block, the 'Boerentoren' (1929–32), at the end of the city's main shopping street, the Meir, designed under the direction of Jan Vanhoenacker.

National pavilions, official presentations and corporate pavilions appeared on the exhibition site. Stynen designed the Pavilion of the Decorative Arts and a pavilion for biscuit manufacturer De Beukelaer. After the exhibition, the grounds were parcelled out and Stynen purchased a plot in this new exhibition district for the construction of his own home, which he moved into in 1933.[8]

After the Second World War, the legendary BP tower, designed by Stynen, emerged at the head of this district, perhaps the most talked-about construction in his oeuvre.

The year 1930 was pivotal for Stynen. His first major project, the Casino in Knokke (1928–30), was built in collaboration with Antwerp architects Jan Vanhoenacker (1875–1958) and François Dens (1880–1968), two elderly master builders whom casino owner Joseph Nellens placed alongside the young Stynen to complete the project in record time. The Casino, with a fully glazed façade facing the sea, became one of Belgium's most important public buildings with a modernist design language and a symbol of the dynamism of this young seaside resort.

In 1931, the Belgian government organized two competitions for a new maritime school, one in Ostend and one in Antwerp. Stynen took part in the former. His perspective drawings show his fascination for Le Corbusier. The attractive drawing of the interior for the school, with many round columns from floor to ceiling, shows an affinity with Le Corbusier's design for the Centrosoyuz complex in Moscow from 1928. The design was published in the first volume of *Le Corbusier. Œuvre complète 1910–29*, a book that Stynen, as an admirer of Le Corbusier, certainly owned. The latter's influence is perhaps most explicitly expressed in Stynen's proposal for the Mohanlal house in Mumbai (1932).

Project for apartment building Mohanlal, Mumbai, 1932

Stynen and the CIAM

The Congrès international d'Architecture moderne (CIAM) was founded in 1928 in La Sarraz, Switzerland. Inspired by Le Corbusier and Sigfried Giedion (1888–1968), it was a response to the direction taken by the design competition for the League of Nations building in Geneva. The judges had opted for a design with a distinctly classical Beaux-Arts design language, and rejected modernist proposals, in particular that of Le Corbusier. The second CIAM meeting took place in 1929 in Frankfurt on the theme of 'Existenzminimum'. In November 1930, the Centre for Fine Arts in Brussels (now BOZAR) was the venue of the congress of the great European avant-garde protagonists. The famous group photo of the meeting shows Ludwig Mies van der Rohe (1886–1969), Le Corbusier and Walter Gropius (1883–1969), as well as other well-known architects from various European countries.

Mies van der Rohe is there not only as an architect, as he had just become director of the Bauhaus after the Hannes Meyer's (1889–1954) resignation in August 1930. In the photo, La Cambre director Henry van de Velde is flanked by Victor Bourgeois, the co-initiator of the CIAM. Absent from the picture is Huib Hoste, who had been forced to resign his appointment in La Cambre after a judicial conviction. Presumably Hoste gave his invitation to 23-year-old Gaston Eysselinck from Ghent, in the centre of the group photo. Hoste regarded Eysselinck as the more talented architect, while he had more reservations about Stynen – this was probably not based on personal considerations but because of the nature of his commissions. In the 1920s, social housing was the central theme for progressive designers. Stynen came into the limelight in 1930 with the exhibition pavilions for Antwerp 1930 and the Knokke Casino.

The secretariat of the Belgian section of CIAM was in the hands of young architects from the aforementioned Liège Groupe L'Équerre, who also published the magazine of the same name.

On the occasion of the *Exposition internationale de l'Eau* in Liège in 1939, the CIAM meeting was supposed to take place there, but it was cancelled due to the threat of war. Participating in the CIAM activities after 1945 (Bridgwater in 1947 to Otterlo in 1959) was no longer a priority for Stynen, as his full attention was then focused on his design and construction of the Casino-Kursaal in Ostend. In 1950, when Stynen was director of the architecture department of the Antwerp Academy, the vice-president of CIAM, architect Ernesto N. Rogers (1909–1969), suggested that he organize a summer school with the AA architecture school in London. Rogers was a partner of the renowned architectural firm BBPR in Milan and editor-in-chief of *Casabella*. He also argued for the promotion of an education committee within the CIAM.

Stynen did stay abreast of the discussions within the CIAM, such as the question of how to arrive at a new architecture that is 'less obsessed with asceticism and nudity'. As early as 1938, Walter Gropius had written a text on this issue, resolutely ruling out a return to ornament and suggesting instead to focus on nature. In 1943, Sigfried Giedion and others argued in 'Nine Points on Monumentality' for the 'return of monumentality' and a collaboration with artists.[9] After 1945, the CIAM paid attention for the first time to the aesthetic aspect and to collaboration with artists.
The relationship between buildings and art was the subject of the exhibition *The Monumental Art*, organized in 1952 in the Brussels Centre for Fine Arts. It presented an overview of twenty years of mural art. The introduction to the accompanying catalogue refers to 'mural aesthetics', the mural art in which the work of art is dependent on the architecture.[10] In almost all examples, the sculptural is reduced to the medium-relief embellishment of the large flat walls of functional architecture. Léon Stynen, just like Gaston Eysselinck, had a different view on this. They believed that architects should provide space for integrated art and radically opposed the 'decorating' of walls. Often the bond between artist and architect was one of friendship or a special appreciation for the work of a contemporary.

Elsdonck residence in *L'Architecture d'aujourd'hui*, no. 10, 1936

Van Thilo private residence in *Le Document d'architecture*, no. 4, 1939

For example, Léon Stynen regularly collaborated with Julien Van Vlasselaer (1907–1982), a teacher at the Antwerp Academy. Many teachers associated with La Cambre also received commissions for artworks for the Kursaal in Ostend.

The 1930s

Two projects for which Stynen also received appreciative mention in the international trade press were Residentie Elsdonck, an apartment building in Wilrijk with spacious residential units (1933), and Hof ten Bos, a sanatorium in Brasschaat (1937).

Stynen built several apartment buildings that fit into the urban fabric. Like many modernists, he preferred buildings in green environments. It is therefore not surprising that Residence Elsdonck was located in such an environment in Wilrijk. Elsdonck is a detached six-storey complex with spacious apartments for a well-to-do bourgeois clientèle.[11] The number of drawings that have come down to us indicate that this was Stynen's first major project after the Knokke Casino. The structure consisted of an all-steel skeleton, a construction method also used for the Boerentoren in Antwerp. The brick façades show nothing of the skeleton. At the rear, facing south, are large terraces, with semi-circular ends. This formal choice also appeared in the oeuvre of German architect Erich Mendelsohn (1887–1953), whom Stynen undoubtedly appreciated and whose work was widely published. In the Schocken department store in Stuttgart (1928), Mendelsohn brought the staircase outside, making it a strong compositional element. The two staircases of Residentie Elsdonck have been brought out in a similar way, giving an expressive aspect to the austere, rectilinear nature of the main volume. Elsdonck was featured in the French architecture magazine *L'Architecture d'aujourd'hui* in 1936, next to the La Warr Pavilion, the casino that Mendelsohn built in collaboration with Serge Chermayeff (1900–1996) at Bexhill-on-Sea on England's south coast. There, too, the expressive volume with the stairs determines the appearance of the building.

The second building that attracted attention to Stynen was a sanatorium built in a wooded area to the north of Antwerp, where children could stay in healthy forest air. At that time, sanatoria were built in Belgium, on the coast, in the Ardennes and also abroad, to combat tuberculosis. With this modernist project, Stynen joined a general tendency to use architecture in a major social challenge for the benefit of public health. The building appeared on the cover of the magazine *Bâtir* (no. 70, 1938). To clarify its destination, there is a child at the bottom right of the photo (see p. 107, top right).

Meanwhile, after Villa Savoye (1928–31), Le Corbusier had moved away from 'dematerializing' his buildings. The complete plastering of his constructions now made way for the use of natural stone. Materials previously described as rustic and traditional were now given a place in modern architecture, signifying a return to the 'tactile' dimension of the materials used, a form of lyrical modernism. Stynen, too, was in search of a different materiality. The Van Thillo house in Ekeren (1936) was faced with dark natural stone from the Belgian Ardennes. The proportions of the natural stone slabs were worked out with great care prior to application. In 1939, Stynen received the Van de Ven architecture prize, the most important award in Belgium, for this doctor's house with practice. This crucial work in Stynen's oeuvre was demolished back in 1977, long before there was any appreciation for the modern heritage. He used the same material in the construction of the Chaudfontaine Casino (1937–38), a project that was rebuilt almost beyond recognition after 1945.

Stynen remained very active during the Depression of the 1930s. Through his extensive network, he was able to build several cinemas in Antwerp and Brussels, which allowed him to further develop his aesthetic preoccupations.

In 1939, Belgium was prominently present at the New York World Fair. Henry van de Velde and the two younger architects Victor Bourgeois and Léon Stynen were allowed to design the Belgian pavilion, but the collaboration did not go so smoothly and Stynen's proposals were rejected.[12] His stay in this city made a big impression. In 1941, he published an article in the magazine *Bouwkunst en wederopbouw* titled 'New York … city full of expectations', illustrated with fifteen photographs, and starting with a quote from Le Corbusier '… New York, projeté[e] avec violence dans le ciel, clameur que l'on hait et que l'on aime tout ensemble, cache au fond des canons des banques, pour qui sait voir, la composition la plus expressive de l'âme du pays' (New York, projected violently into the sky, a clamour that one hates and loves simultaneously, hides, at the bottom of the banks' canons for those who know how to look, the composition most expressive of the soul of the country).[13]

Collaboration with Paul De Meyer
For an architect wanting to build, the Second World War must have been a very frustrating time, but Stynen was able to concentrate on his teaching assignment. From 1939 to 1945, he taught at the Academy of Antwerp, where from 1946 he was Director of the Department of Architecture. However, his archive shows that already in 1942 he was in contact with Gustave Nellens, a scion of the Nellens family for whom he had also built the casinos of Knokke and Chaudfontaine. That year, the German occupier demolished the monumental Kursaal complex erected in Ostend by architect Alban Chambon (1847–1928) in order to build a bunker on this prime location. In 1944, even before the end of the war, Stynen, at Nellens' request, made a detailed proposal for its reconstruction, with dozens of drawings and a model. In September 1945, after the liberation, the city council decided to organize a competition. Stynen was certainly disappointed that he would not be able to present his existing proposal, presumably on Nellens' advice. However, the study work gave him a considerable advantage over the other participants. In June 1946, Stynen won the competition, subject to certain adjustments. His situation was delicate – the city of Ostend was both the client and the issuer of the building permit.

With this assignment, Stynen understood that he would need to give his architectural firm a new structure. During his visit to America in 1939, he probably became acquainted with the development of professional agencies to win large orders and to bring them to a successful conclusion. He needed to form a partnership, and his choice fell on the young architect Paul De Meyer (1922–2011), son of the Liers architect Bernard De Meyer. Paul De Meyer – eighteen when the Second World War broke out – had studied at the Royal Academy of Fine Arts in Antwerp, including with Stynen, and graduated in 1944. The restructuring of his office also gave Stynen the opportunity to aspire to other positions, such as the directorship of La Cambre in Brussels and the chair of the Order of Architects. De Meyer became his permanent partner in 1947 and remained so until Stynen ended his professional career in 1977.

A skilful and faithful right hand was necessary to run the studio. Stynen probably had in mind the example of Le Corbusier's studio in the Rue de Sèvres in Paris, where Pierre Jeanneret, Le Corbusier's cousin, was a partner. Stynen attracted other young

Léon Stynen and Paul De Meyer

talents and gave them opportunities, among them Walter Bresseleers (1927–1980) and Paul Meekels (°1929), who later successfully started their own practices. With the design of his penthouse at the top of the Riverside Tower on Antwerp's Left Bank (1967–72), Paul De Meyer showed himself to be a full-fledged partner with design talent and technical competence.[14]

The opening of the Ostend Kursaal in 1953 marked the end of a story that started in 1944. At about the same time, the PTT/RTT building was also erected in Ostend, the masterpiece of architect Gaston Eysselinck.[15] Both architects shared a mutual appreciation and Eysselinck realized that the new Kursaal would have a different function than before 1940: 'In our time, with our democratic views, I cannot imagine or establish the meaning of a Casino other than as a giant cosmopolitan people's house, and let us shout loudly at the majority: we are convinced that we are right, for, in this vision, what could not emanate as good and educational from a casino!' In 1948, Eysselinck reiterated this point of view.[16]

Extra space was needed to further develop the Stynen and De Meyer practice. It moved into the residential and office complex De Zonnewijzer, for which the practice had made an initial design in 1954 and which was erected on the edge of the Koning Albertpark in Antwerp. This marked a break in the long tradition of combining architect's studio and home.

The office did not receive many assignments for social housing. In the 1950s, it contributed to the Casablanca garden city in Kessel-Lo, the urban plan of which was designed by Victor Bourgeois. In the Koning Albert building (1955–60) of the garden city, Stynen and De Meyer introduced duplex apartments. It was recently decided to demolish this building.

Glass or concrete

In several interviews, Stynen stressed that one of his preoccupations in the period 1945–53 was to avoid making mistakes in the execution of his largest project to date, the Ostend Kursaal. It had to prove that he could handle large projects and also that he possessed the requisite technical skills. His attitude was very similar to that of Gaston Eysselinck, who was then working on the PTT/RTT building.

For the façades of the Kursaal in Ostend, whose skeleton was made of concrete, Stynen opted for white natural stone. Using concrete on the outside was too risky owing to the aggressive, salty sea air. As in the Knokke Casino, he aimed for a grand view of the sea, resulting in high, glazed façade sections, a double construction with an aluminium framework on the outside and steel profiles on the inside. In the intervening space, Stynen used horizontal Vierendeel trusses to give the façade stability, but also permit optimal window cleaning. In such details, Stynen showed his construction engineering skill. The fact that the large, glazed façades were not damaged during the massive storm in the winter of 1953 only confirms this.

The glass curtain wall made its appearance in modern architecture with iconic buildings in New York, like the UN headquarters designed by architects Gordon Bunshaft/SOM (1950–52), and with the many designs elsewhere by Mies van der Rohe in the 1950s. It had a major impact on the appearance of buildings. Natural materials and brick were omitted and replaced by double glazing and aluminium façade profiles. Stynen and De Meyer's post-1945 work points to a lack of affinity with the work of Van der Rohe and those architects who evolved towards an arid modernity and the new trend of curtain walls. For the Kursaal specifically, Stynen opted for the glazed façade, but in this case to obtain an optimal view of the sea.

Stynen favoured lyrical modernism with a clear preference for concrete. The only building he built with an extremely light façade is the BP building, a total concept with suspended floors and façades.

Ronchamp and Harelbeke

In 1955, the Notre-Dame du Haut chapel in Ronchamp, a magnificent creation by Le Corbusier, was consecrated. In Catholic circles the chapel was met with great surprise: how could an unconvinced Catholic even design a church? Le Corbusier's opponents considered him a communist or a Bolshevik after he built the Centrosoyuz complex in Moscow in 1928. However, the Dominicans had an open mind and gave him the opportunity to give this pilgrimage site on a hill a new dimension. Later, he also built a monastery near Lyon.

Stynen was not a Catholic, but a member of a Masonic lodge. The first sketches for the Sint-Rita church in Harelbeke, consecrated in 1966, date from 1957. They were made by André Vlieghe, a local architect. Since they did not meet the requirements, in the spring of 1958 Stynen's practice was brought in. Paul Meekels and Paul De Meyer then worked out a proposal, a church with sloping roofs, resembling a large

St Rita's Church, Harelbeke, 1966

Pantheon, Rome

barn. In early 1959, the design process took a drastic turn when Stynen took over. 'In Harelbeke, the tent shape of the building is like a pyramid', wrote Albert Bontridder when discussing this exceptional project.[17] Whence came the inspiration? Perhaps the name of the neighbourhood – Zandberg – was reminiscent of an upturned bucket in front of a sandcastle. An important factor, however, was Expo '58 in Brussels, for which Stynen and De Meyer had also carried out a number of commissions. One of the high-profile creations at the world fair was the *Pijl van de Burgerlijke Bouwkunde* or *Flèche du Génie civil* (Arrow of Civil Architecture), a pavilion by architects Jean Van Doosselaere (1919–2000) and Jacques Moeschal (1913–2004) and especially the work of engineer and ULB professor André Paduart (1914–1985). Does the choice of Paduart for the concrete construction in Harelbeke have anything to do with Stynen's original ambition to do engineering studies?

The church of Harelbeke is often compared to the Saint-Pierre designed by Le Corbusier in Firminy, France. However, Stynen insisted that the source of inspiration was not that church, but rather Le Corbusier's parliament building in Chandigarh in India. Stynen may also have wanted to make a modern version of the Pantheon in Rome, something every architect dreams of. He wanted to transfer this building of classical architecture – a temple and later a church, a space without windows but with an opening at the top to let in the zenithal light – to the twentieth century. Between the 1959 design and its completion in 1966, the exterior shape of the church remained unchanged, while the interior was radically adapted to the new liturgical practices following the Second Vatican Council.

C&A store, Ghent, 1965-66

Galler, Antwerp, 1961–63

One client, seven buildings

C&A (an abbreviation of Clemens & August Brenninkmeijer) was originally a Dutch clothing chain and before 1940 had many branches in the Netherlands, Germany and England. In the 1950s, the family decided to expand into the Belgian market. Land was purchased in the main Belgian shopping streets to erect new buildings. C&A opened its stores in Belgium in record time: Antwerp (1963), Hasselt (1963–64), Brussels (1963–65), Ghent (1965–66), Kortrijk (1966–67), Sint-Lambrechts-Woluwe (1968), Namur (1969), Charleroi (1967–69) and Bruges (1969–70). Nine new C&A branches in seven years: this was only possible by entrusting the assignments to one architectural firm, Stynen and De Meyer, and the execution to one contracting company, Van Coillie from Ostend. Seven C&A stores had similar exteriors, but differences due to the specificity of the location and the dimensions of the lot. The C&A store in Sint-Lambrechts-Woluwe was part of the new Woluwe Shopping Center, while in Bruges the existing façades of three buildings were retained and restored.

Before 1940, department stores had façades with a lot of glass and a central light well to bring in daylight. With the arrival of better electric lighting after 1945, and especially the TL lamp, the need for daylight within the retail space was drastically reduced. The central atrium, the model for a large urban shop from the nineteenth century, disappeared and was replaced by escalators.

What remained was the demand for ground floor display space to present the products. Department stores now also had closed façade surfaces, with architects expected to provide compositional answers. Marcel Breuer (1902–1981) had done this for the Bijenkorf in Rotterdam by embellishing the closed façade with the store's logo.

Instead of opting for closed surfaces, Stynen and De Meyer decided to rhythm the concrete façades in order to achieve a softer integration into the streetscapes. The first C&A store in Antwerp was located on a wide plot along the Meir next to the Stadsfeestzaal with its monumental façade. Stynen understood that he could not propose a closed façade in this context. He had to be inventive and find a different solution for this large new building volume. The source of inspiration was the solution that modernists, especially Le Corbusier, came up with: a brise-soleil.

In the long façade of the C&A store in Antwerp, a protruding volume was created in the form of a large window onto the city, facing the other side of the street. There stood the magnificent Osterrieth House, designed by the great eighteenth-century Antwerp master builder Jan Pieter van Baurscheidt the Younger. Stynen must have thought that two great Antwerp architects faced each other. The old building was restored under the impulse of Maurits Naessens, banker, humanist and friend of Stynen.

Even before the C&A commissions, Stynen had erected two other buildings in Antwerp in which the rhythm of the concrete façade was carefully designed: the L'Assurance liegeoise office building (1960–62) and the Galler trading complex (1961–63). The façades of the C&A stores in Ghent and Kortrijk were similarly composed with compact grid patterns, while the one in Charleroi was much more austere. The C&A store fronts in Brussels, Antwerp and Ghent had presentation or display cabinets at the entrance, the height of which was lower than that of the ground floor retail area. Over the years, these display cases disappeared and were replaced by glass surfaces running the full height.

In fact, the brief was to create as large a sales area and as few columns as possible to allow for an adaptable arrangement of textile products. Stynen & De Meyer produced some designs for the insides of the shops, but the interior design was primarily developed by the C&A group itself.

The golden sixties
The 1960s were extremely busy years for architects. The economy grew strongly and commissions came in quickly. It was a period of belief in expansion, in growth without limits. The dilapidated inner cities had to be tackled, but little importance was attached to heritage value and buildings were demolished at lightning speed. Major works were necessary for a new future. To give new life to cities, major urban works were launched to improve accessibility for car traffic, and work was done on new commercial and cultural infrastructure. Old buildings needed to make way for new constructions, which had a major impact on the urban fabric. What we now regard as important historical patrimony laid the groundwork for large-scale new construction that was required to express faith in the future.

Fortunately, many proposals got no further than the project stage. In 1961, Le Corbusier made a design for a large cultural centre on the Seine in Paris that was combined with the Aérogare d'Orly, a connection to Orly airport. To do this, the Gare d'Orsay, built for the great World's Fair of 1900, had to be demolished. New large-scale programmes were also designed in Belgium, involving the demolition of what we now regard as architectural heritage. Stynen and De Meyer were involved in such ambitious plans in Antwerp and Ghent at the initiative of banker Maurits Naessens. In Ghent, the nineteenth-century opera house had to be demolished to make way for a cultural centre and offices. Stynen also worked out an alternative that retained the opera house. The ancient Ketelvest, the connection between the rivers Leie and Scheldt, was filled in to make way for the car. An elegant tower accentuated this new city development.

BP Tower, Antwerp, 1959-63

Three buildings next to each other
Located close to each other along the Antwerp ring road are three striking creations by Stynen and De Meyer: the BP office building (1959–63), the Esso Motor Hotel (1969) and, on the other side of the ring road, the Royal Flemish Music Conservatory (1962–87). The practice devised many projects for this site, including the Wezenberg urbanization plan (1962–72).

Esso Motor Hotel, Antwerp, 1969

Stynen and De Meyer sought architectural elegance. BP building has a special expression due to its suspended construction. The Esso Motor Hotel, now the Crowne Plaza, was built at about the same time as the Riverside Tower on the Left Bank. The façade composition has a three-part division on each floor, in contrast to the frequently used two-part solution with a solid surface and a window section. The effect was to visually reduce the scale of the building volume. The design has some affinity with that of Japanese architect Kenzō Tange (1913–2005) for the Fiera complex in Bologna, designed in 1967 but not inaugurated until 1983.

Music Conservatory, Antwerp, 1962-87

How do you go about designing a conservatory, a place where young people and teachers come together for music education? For the site of the new building, the land of the second city belt was chosen. Located in a green zone, it would unfortunately be occupied by the motorway around Antwerp and a train track. The first phase (1962–80) consisted of the construction of the classroom and rehearsal rooms, structured around two inner gardens. It evoked a monastic community, for whom life had been organized around an inner garden for centuries. Similarly, the former La Cambre abbey in Brussels, where the École de La Cambre is housed and Stynen was director, was a monastery complex in a green oasis, structured around inner gardens.

The vestibule of the Conservatory is special. A wide, autonomously placed staircase is perpendicular to the entrance doors. The slight slope of the staircase is reminiscent of the freestanding staircase designed by Andrea Palladio in the sixteenth century for the convent of San Giorgio in Venice. Leading from the corridor to the refectory, it is clear evidence of Stynen's knowledge of classical architecture. Most striking are the organically shaped openings in the concrete walls near the stairs, an obvious reference to Le Corbusier's parliament building in Chandigarh. In 1963, Stynen had travelled to the new city in northern India designed by Le Corbusier. He had taken photographs there, a number of prints of which he donated to Le Corbusier in appreciation.

Riverside Tower, Antwerp, Stynen and De Meyer, 1969

Fieracomplex, Bologna, architect Kenzō Tange, 1967

Construction of the Conservatory took place in three phases and was eventually combined with the establishment of the deSingel international arts centre. At the beginning of the twenty-first century, the complex was expanded according to a design by architect Stéphane Beel (°1955).

Buildings constructed in concrete are often catalogued under the term 'brutalism'. Wikipedia describes this as 'a movement within architecture which originated from modernism. It is characterized by often large block-like structures of rough unfinished reinforced concrete or brickwork'. The term is etymologically related to 'brutal', a characteristic that certainly does not radiate from Stynen and De Meyer's work. No doubt both would have been shocked by this description since their attitude as designers was to seek architectural elegance. 'Lyrical modernism' thus seems to be a better description of their work, or 'elegant concrete'.

International renown

Stynen understood that joining an association that championed the ideas of modern architecture could position him. Yet, in the 1930s, he was not a member of the Société belge des Urbanistes et Architectes modernistes (SBUAM), founded in 1923, which brought together architects from Wallonia, Flanders and Brussels.[18] Perhaps he wanted to profile himself in Antwerp and contribute to an organization that emphasized good master-building skills. He became a member of the Koninklijke Maatschappij der Bouwmeesters van Antwerpen (Royal Society of Antwerp Master-Builders (KMBA), the oldest association of master builders in Belgium, founded in 1848. The first issue of the monthly magazine *K.M.B.A. Maandschrift voor bouwkunst en aanverwante vakken* was published in June 1930.

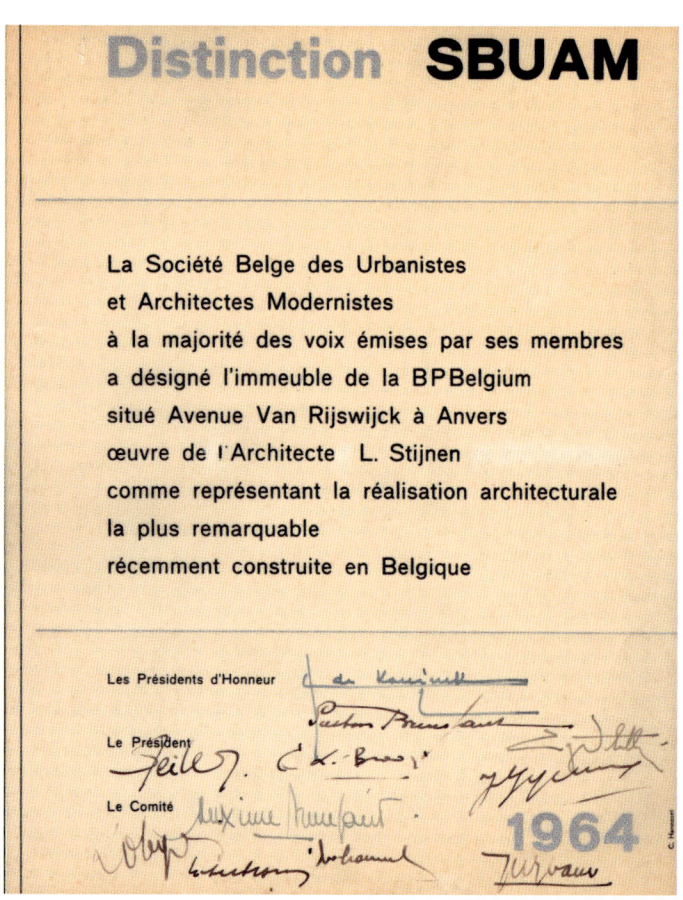

SBUAM Distinction for the BP Building, 1964

Unrealized project for the Antwerp National Contemporary Arts Museum based on a project by Le Corbusier (1939), 1968

It contained the Decorative Arts Pavilion, which Stynen had designed for the World's Fair then taking place in Antwerp. He later joined the editorial board. In number 3 of March 1937, his own house, where he had been living since in 1933, appeared with six illustrations. In the second half of the 1930s, the number of building commissions had dwindled and perhaps he hoped for new orders with the publication. To get his work published internationally, the Brussels connection was necessary. This was facilitated by Victor Bourgeois.

In 1936, Belgium was one of the ten countries invited to take part in 'Nuova Architettura nel Mondo', the fifth Milan Triennale, under the direction of Giuseppe Pagano and Edoardo Persico.[19] The exhibition included a voluminous reference work with 650 images, published by Ulrico Hoepli in Milan. Except for Léon Stynen, all participating Belgian architects were from Brussels. The selection was made by Victor Bourgeois.

In Italy, three editions were also published of the standard work compiled by Alberto Sartoris, *Gli elementi dell'architettura funzionale* (1932, 1935 and 1941). The second and third editions include the work of Gaston Eysselinck, but not Stynen. The accompanying photographs were provided to the author by Huib Hoste, demonstrating that Bourgeois and Hoste formed a link in disseminating the work of Belgian architects internationally.

After 1945, a panorama of Belgian architecture was presented during Expo '58 in Brussels. However, the number of initiatives to put Belgian architecture on the international map remained small. The SBUAM, which remained active after 1945, gave Stynen and De Meyer a special award in 1964 for the BP tower building in Antwerp. A year later, in the buildings of the Order of Catalan Architects in Barcelona, the *Arquitectura Belga de hoy* exhibition was held, which brought Belgium to the public's attention. The short text accompanying this exhibition was written by architect Pierre Puttemans (1933–2013). Of the twenty-six invited architects, two were from Flanders: Jamagne & Van der Elst and Léon Stynen (without mention of De Meyer).

In 1979, *Gevecht met de rede:* Léon *Stynen, leven en werk (Fight with reason: Léon Stynen, life and work)* was published on the occasion of Stynen's eightieth birthday. It was written by his friend, architect and poet Albert Bontridder.[20] This publication, printed in Dutch and French, was distributed by the Léon Stynen Committee and hardly made it into bookshops. Unfortunately, this first book about Stynen contributed little to bringing greater exposure to his oeuvre, either in Belgium or internationally.

In 1990, the year of his death, the deSingel arts centre organized its first major exhibition dedicated to Stynen. The entire building, both deSingel and the music conservatory, formed the framework for the presentation of his extensive legacy. The accompanying large-format publication missed the opportunity to place Stynen in an international context.[21] The author, Geert Bekaert, had shown little appreciation for Stynen's work in the past.

It was not until 2018 that a full-fledged retrospective was presented by the VAi/Flemish Architecture Institute, and also organized in one of Stynen and De Meyer's crucial projects, deSingel. The choice to publish the accompanying publication in English was intended to present the work to an international audience. A second edition has already appeared in 2023. Several authors were brought together to study and publish the work from different angles and themes. This also shows the diversity of Stynen's work, from urban planning to furniture.

Interior designs as fully-fledged assignments
Over the years, Stynen and De Meyer paid a lot of attention to interior decoration commissions, including for hotels, boats and trains. Before 1940, Stynen was involved in the interior design of the *Baudouinville,* the ship that connected Belgium and the Belgian Congo. In 1955, another ship followed, the *King Leopold III* for the connection Ostend-Dover. The practice was also involved in the design of the new TEE trainsets for the Amsterdam–Paris connection (1963).

After 1945, the supply of modern furniture was plentiful and of good quality. For example, the well-known De Coene company in Kortrijk acquired the licence to produce and sell the collection of the American firm Knoll International. Herman Miller's creations also entered the Belgian market. The Belgian company Tubax, moreover, produced the furniture designs of Willy Van der Meeren (1923–2002) from 1945 onwards. Stynen designed a chair for Expo '58 in Brussels, which was produced by Antwerp company Straatman, Loral & Cie. That chair graced the cover of the June 1960 edition of the magazine *Bouwen en wonen*. It became widely, even internationally, known when the Bulo company from Mechelen successfully relaunched the design under the name SL 58.

1 Dirk Laureys (ed.), *Léon Stynen. A Life of Architecture 1899–1990*, exh. cat., Antwerp, Flanders Architecture Institute, 2018; Maurice Culot and François Terlinden, *Antoine Pompe et l'effort moderne en Belgique 1890–1940*, exh. cat., Elsene, Musée d'Ixelles, 1969, pp. 167–168; Geert Bekaert and Francis Strauven, *Bouwen in België 1945–1970*, Brussels, Nationale Confederatie van het Bouwbedrijf, 1971; Dirk Laureys, 'Stynen, Léon', in: Anne Van Loo (ed.), *Repertory of Architecture in Belgium from 1830 to the Present*, Antwerp, Mercatorfonds, 2003, pp. 523–525.
2 Le Corbusier, *Kommende Baukunst*, Stuttgart/Berlin/Leipzig, Deutsche Verlags-Anstalt, 1926.
3 Marc Dubois, 'Leiden-Antwerpen-(Brugge)-Paris. Architect Mallet-Stevens en de relatie met België en Nederland', in: *Interbellum*, XXV, 5 (2005), pp. 7–15.
4 Phillip Van den Bossche, Adriaan Gonnissen, Saki Mafundikwa et al., *Flouquet, Kassák, Léonard. De architectuur van het beeld tijdens het interbellum / The Architecture of Images During the Interwar Period*, Ostend, Mu.ZEE, 2018.
5 Pierre-Louis Flouquet, 'L'architecture moderne en Flandre', in: *Bâtir*, 8 (1933), pp. 281–285, interview with Huib Hoste. The article also includes a photo of Stynen's pavilion for the World's Fair for Colonies, Maritime and Flemish Art in Antwerp in 1930.
6 Albert Bontridder, *La raison revoltée: Léon Stynen, sa vie et son œuvre / Gevecht met de rede: Léon Stynen, leven en werk*, Antwerp, Comité Léon Stynen, 1979, p. 60.
7 Jacques Aron, *La Cambre et l'architecture: un regard sur le Bauhaus belge*, Brussels, Pierre Mardaga, 1982; Jacques Aron, Pierre Puttemans, Albert Bontridder, Henry van de Velde and Paul Émile Vincent, *Les Architectes qui ont fait La Cambre* (Les Cahiers de La Cambre - Architecture, 2), Brussels, Institut supérieur d'Architecture de l'État La Cambre (ISAE), 1985.
8 Willem Van Zadelhoff, 'Een manier van leven, een manier van bouwen. Het eigen woonhuis van Léon Stynen', in: *Monumenten & Landschappen*, 4 (1997), pp. 41–56. House Stynen was also featured in the magazine *KMBA*, no. 3, March 1937.
9 Josep Lluís Sert, Fernand Léger and Sigfried Giedion, 'Nine Points on Monumentality (1943)', in: Joan Ockman and Edward Eigen (eds.), *Architecture-Culture, 1945–1968: A Documentary Anthology*, New York, Rizzoli, 1993, p. 29–30.
10 Lucien Christophe, 'Inleiding', in *De monumentale kunst in de openbare en industriële gebouwen: tentoonstelling ingericht door het Ministerie van Openbaar Onderwijs*, exh. cat., Brussels, Connaissance, 1952.
11 Anne Malliet, 'Résidence Elsdonck, een opmerkelijk en kleurig appartementsgebouw, oorspronkelijk in het groen', in: *Monumenten & Landschappen*, 4 (1996), pp. 22–34.
12 Dirk Laureys, *Léon Stynen, op. cit.*, p. 19.
13 Léon Stynen, 'New York … stad vol verwachting', in: *Bouwkunst en wederopbouw*, 9 (September 1941), pp. 221–236.
14 Marc Dubois, *Riverside Tower Antwerpen. Iconische woontoren door Stynen and De Meyer*, Ghent, Artha Books, 2022.
15 Marc Dubois, *Gaston Eysselinck 1907–1953. In the Footsteps of Le Corbusier*, Ghent, Snoeck, 2019.
16 Gaston Eysselinck, in the column 'Kroniek van de wederopbouw' in *Voor allen*, 36 (1948): 'The casino, regardless of the financial difficulties involved in its construction, the form in which it has been conceived seems to me to be a very sympathetic solution of a giant people's house in which the industrial branch of the gaming is cleverly linked in a subtle way…'
17 Albert Bontridder, *op. cit.*
18 Pierre Bourgeois, Pierre Verbruggen and R. Vanderborght, *SBUAM: historique, activité, membres*, Brussels, Éditions La Cité, 1938. In 1938 eight architects from Ghent were members of the SBUAM, and only three from Antwerp (Huib Hoste, Constant Leurs and Jozef Ritzen).
19 Giuseppe Pagano and Agnoldomenico Pica, *Nuova architettura nel mondo*, Milan, Hoepli, 1938. Presumably the selection had gone through Victor Bourgeois. The book contains several country pavilions (Switzerland, Austria, Czechoslovakia) from the 1935 World's Fair in Brussels.
20 Albert Bontridder, *op. cit.*, p. 60.
21 Geert Bekaert and Ronny De Meyer, *Léon Stynen, een architect. Antwerpen 1899–1990*, Antwerp, deSingel, 1990.

Holiday home I Tre Cipressi, Gargnano, 1957

Stynen planted three cypress trees, symbolizing his belief in reason, beauty and wisdom, the three basic principles that architecture needs to incarnate, according to Vitruvius.

THE TEACHER & LA CAMBRE

PABLO LHOAS

La Cambre, homage to architect Victor Bourgeois

Léon Stynen by Lucien De Roeck

Ecole Nationale Supérieure d'Architecture et des Arts Décoratifs, ENSAAD (La Cambre) New Year's greetings card by Lucien De Roeck, 1955

Léon Stynen and typography teacher Lucien De Roeck, 1965

Victor Bourgeois, François (Francis) Jamagne and Léon Stynen

King Baudouin visits La Cambre, 1962

Princess Paola visits La Cambre, 1964

With Camille Huysmans (in the centre)

Léon Stynen, Directeur de l'Ecole Nationale Supérieure d'Architecture et des Arts Décoratifs « La Cambre » Bruxelles achève sa mission en 1964. Il vous souhaite, ainsi que Marie-Jeanne, une année nouvelle faite de bonheur et d'espérance

Jean Styrnas.
Eloquence de l'Architecture

Amitié Commune   Amsterdam 13 Novembre 1972
Chapitre.   .   Mons 10 Mai 1973.

At the age of 73, Léon Stynen conceived the idea of composing a kind of 'philosophical-architectural testament'. This explains the high level and ambition of this text, in which he not only uses 'definitive' definitions of architecture – developed very methodically based on history – but also seeks to present architecture in the context of a moral vision and major values.

It is one of the rare texts of its kind that Léon Stynen wrote - which is perhaps why he put so much emphasis on it! Stynen knew architecture through and through: he not only practised and taught it, but he also headed two schools of architecture – the Royal Academy of Antwerp and La Cambre, the anti-academy that Henry van de Velde founded in Brussels in 1928. He was intimately involved in the greatest (r)evolutions of twentieth century architecture. He was close personally to the leading figures – Van de Velde, Le Corbusier, Ernesto Nathan Rogers, and others – who gave shape to the modernist architectural revolution. He also played a role as an architect, a militant of the modern cause. He was close to the international congresses on modern architecture – the famous CIAMs, where between 1928 and 1959 the modern doctrine was established and later developed by the new Team X generation. He also played a direct role in this process through his CIAM-related tasks and his teaching.

It is somewhat surprising, therefore, that this advocate of rationalism, abstract architecture, anti-historicism and a certain architectural functionalism speaks in this text in almost mystical terms. His reflections are rooted in morality, but also history and the idea that architecture is a language that is not just highly expressive, but value-based. We should not forget, however, that Stynen was constantly aware of modern architecture and society and the evolution of both. This text attests to this: written in 1972 and revised the following year, it displays the influence of theorists and historians who were sceptics of modernity and even became advocates of postmodernity. John Summerson (*The Classical Language of Architecture*, 1963) was one of the first, followed by Charles Jencks ('Semiology and Architecture' in the collective work *Meaning in Architecture*, 1969).

The 1960s challenged the modernist dogma, which had – in the inter-war period – been radical, rebellious and avant-garde at first, and afterwards became dominant, tamed, and institutional. This was the beginning of a productive period of crisis. Radical architecture, post-modern architecture, neo-rationalist architecture, and the architects of the New York Five, among others, challenged the convictions of the fathers of the first modernity, whose heroic heir was Léon Stynen. As architect, militant, and educator, he was, of course, the strong and powerful embodiment of an established generation against which the students in the early 1960s fought. Nonetheless, the end of Stynen's text shows in part his relationship to technology and nature and that he was very aware of the architectural and social trends of his time.

— 1 —

Is it not paradoxical to invoke moral and spiritual values, after decades of campaigning for rational architecture? Do functionalism/ rationalism and mysticism make good bedfellows?

" VALEURS SPIRITUELLES DE L'ARCHITECTURE "

" ELOQUENCE DE L'ARCHITECTURE "

How should we view the return to expressiveness after decades of abstract architecture?

Rigour and method: explaining what is to be developed – always welcome!

a) Exposé
b) L'architecture et son espace
c) Langage de l'architecture
d) Exemples historiques
e) Conclusion - Notre temps

Grasping the themes of his time! Still very topical, also today – and in education – how can we help to tackle the enormous challenges of society and architecture?

Relying on history to justify his words – like Le Corbusier? (in *Vers une architecture*?) – and at the same time 'denigrating' the shortcomings of architects' misuse of the history of their trade, especially by those of the nineteenth century?

Also this form of precision: the date of the text and the indication of the changes testify to Léon Stynen's rational and mind and sense of precision.

Anvers 13 novembre 1972

Mons 10 mai 1973.

– 2 –

Today we might add 'technology' to this – art, science and technology – but it is still very current as the 'definition' of architecture.

. Exposé .

Art et Science à la fois, l'architecture ne traduit-elle pas le plus parfaitement, le plus fidèlement, le caractère des époques qui jalonnent l'histoire?

This can never be said enough and architecture is kept at a distance, when it should be shared more – also with non-architects!

Sous les formes abstraites dont elle se revêt, n'est-ce pas elle qui nous apprend non seulement comment vivent et vivaient des hommes, mais aussi quels sont ou quels étaient leur idéal, leurs inquiétudes et leurs espérances.

C'est pourquoi, plutôt que de parler des valeurs

A big 'problem' that we have inherited from the modern movement is what I would dare call the 'fear' of talking about shapes – because of the shapes themselves and what they say, because they also say things.

formelles des édifices anciens ou actuels, mon intention est de signifier l'accord qui existe, entre l'architecture et les valeurs morales d'une société. Autrement dit, je tenterai d'expliquer en quoi l'architecture plus qu'objet esthétique, est le reflet des aspirations spirituelles, le miroir des soucis matériels de ceux qui au travers de l'histoire, l'ont créé et réalisée. Nous verrons

In the interval between the original text and his subsequent corrections, Léon Stynen has become somewhat more 'cautious' in his statements.

alors comment l'architecture actuelle, déjà donne la mesure des valeurs de notre monde et quelle [pourrait être] ~~sera~~ la qualité de son message.

o o o o o

L'architecture et son espace

Attributing narrative and poetic qualities to architecture may not have been self-evident for Stynen, who was trained in functionalism. But here he follows the trajectory of one of his main inspirations, Le Corbusier, who also took this path in the course of his career. Compare, for example, the Villa Savoye with the Chapel of Ronchamps - and in his texts - *Vers une architecture* in 1923 with *Poème de l'angle droit* in 1955. Not always evident in current architectural education, where recognition of the narrative aspect is strongly present – and then more via metatexts – but that of poetry much less so. As if the current challenges of architecture left no room for that aspect. Pity!

> Disserter sur les qualités narratives et poétiques de l'architecture, c'est parler du prestige de la forme construite et de l'influence de l'espace architectural sur l'esprit humain. Mais disons tout d'abord que l'architecture telle qu'elle évolue depuis la fin du XVIIIe siècle, n'apporte guère de satisfaction aux besoins spirituels de l'homme et même combien elle lui est étrangère.
>
> Cependant, personne ne peut nier que la production architecturale, quelque soit le moment de sa réalisation, exige un apport vivant où l'action de l'universel se confond avec celle du sentiment. Même si à l'époque actuelle la présence de l'art dans la vie n'est pas appréciée, il reste que l'architecture seule parmi les arts, est une réalité qui s'impose, réalité très éloignée de la gratuité et de la spéculation, si fréquentes dans le domaine de la peinture ou de la sculpture.

Here, too, the new text is more direct, more up-front and stronger ... for someone who has always been a fierce defender of art in general and, we must not forget, who has directed schools in which architecture, painting, sculpture, fine art, industrial aesthetics ... existed side-by-side.

A bit high-flying in order to make his point. But resonating curiously with certain radical – anti-modernist – forms of architecture active in that period, in particular with the project of the Italian Superstudio group – published in 1971–72, thus in the same period as this text – entitled 'The fundamental acts: Life, Education, Ceremony, Love, Death'.

Fifty years on, the issue still resonates as much, and as heirs of La Cambre we still strive to speak not only from architect to architect, but to fight for a wider, non-elitist dissemination of architectural culture and for the sharing of architecture.

This too could have been written today. We are still trying to mobilize as wide an audience as possible for themes like urban planning and architecture. We seek to reconcile everyone with responsibility for 'making the city', to make everything more fluid, more correct, more relevant and better shared in the common interest and not for the satisfaction of individual interests.

- 4 -

L'architecture est le reflet de la vie, l'expression des heures vécues, de l'enfance à la mort. Que nous le voulions ou non, les actes courants ou exceptionnels de l'existence s'inscrivent inéluctablement dans ses formes, comme d'ailleurs s'insinuent dans son espace, non seulement les signes de la vie, mais aussi fatalement, ceux de l'indifférence et de l'abandon. *hélas* !

A ce sujet je me suis posé la question:

Dans quelle mesure, le public désire-t-il s'intéresser à l'architecture?

Je ne parle pas de l'architecture élément de culture, mais plus simplement de l'architecture élément actif du milieu urbain, dans lequel s'organise et se déroule la vie quotidienne. Croyez que ce problème me laisse perplexe, sachant combien sont surprenantes l'incompréhension et l'indifférence de beaucoup, devant les édifices anciens les plus émouvants, ou les constructions actuelles les plus remarquables; combien aussi, le public reste quasi sans réaction, devant le spectacle que présente le développement dramatique des villes et l'altération profonde des campagnes et des sites.

Nothing has changed!

Cette situation me tourmente et je comprends mal pourquoi, l'architecture contrairement aux autres arts, retient si peu l'attention alors qu'elle est, je le répète, une des expressions les plus directes des activités de l'homme et une des manifestations les plus éloquentes de sa condition, celle-là même, dont l'homme de la préhistoire déjà, donna le témoignage lorsqu'il creusa son premier abri, inscrivant dans le relief rocheux les images qui hantaient ses rêves et nourrissaient son espoir.

L'architecture, à la fois matière et esprit, forme et contenu, demande de ceux qui souhaitent la comprendre, que la même attention soit accordée aux fonctions matérielles et affectives de la forme qu'aux buts spirituels contenus dans son espace. Le caractère abstrait de ces données et par conséquent de ses représentations, déroute et ne rend pas l'approche de l'architecture facile. Si les buts spirituels contenus dans l'espace sont difficiles à percevoir, parce que suggérés uniquement par un certain dimensionnement, par le jeu de la lumière et le mouvement des ombres, par le mystère des sons qui passent et se dérobent, les raisons inscrites dans les formes, par contre, se découvrent plus aisément, celles-ci étant exprimées par la matière, par les valeurs chromatiques, le rythme et l'harmonie.

We almost hear Le Corbusier himself here and his definition of architecture in the famous *Vers une architecture* from 1923.

And look, here he too is talking about technology, in addition to art and science!

According to some traditions – like the one Léon Stynen invokes at the very end of the text? – the geometrician stands for wisdom and strength. To which the architect can help add beauty.

A debate that is still very much alive. Among other things, in the unfortunately still-existent 'rivalry' between engineer and architect – also in education. Even if architecture is now also a university course: the Higher Institute of Architecture of the French-speaking Community, La Cambre, was separated in 1980 from the institution that succeeded the Higher School of Decorative Arts founded by Henry van de Velde, and merged with the Institut supérieur d'Architecture Victor Horta, part of the former Académie des Beaux-Arts. In this way, the Faculty of Architecture La Cambre Horta of the ULB was created in 2009.

N'empêche que c'est la somme de ces valeurs qui confère à l'architecture, outre son potentiel esthétique, son éloquence et son pouvoir poétique. Conjointement à ces valeurs, la technique de son côté intervient puissamment dans la réalisation et l'expression architecturale; à tel point, qu'une oeuvre ne peut susciter l'admiration et l'enthousiasme, que dans la mesure où la construction répond correctement aux règles de la stabilité, et traduit aussi parfaitement les tensions qui s'opèrent dans les matériaux mis en oeuvre.

Cela est important et les grandes réalisations architecturales, reconnues pour leur plénitude et leur rayonnement, témoignent de cette vérité.

Les effets de la construction s'expriment toujours dans l'architecture, mais la construction comme telle reste la construction, et si par hasard, elle s'élève au degré de l'architecture, comme c'est le cas pour certains travaux de génie civil, c'est qu'au delà du seul souci de construire, l'ingénieur a inscrit dans les formes techniques outre la véracité de son raisonnement, une intention plus subtile et plus humaine.

> **This could/should become more and more topical as technical regulations – sustainability… – weigh heavy in architectural design and therefore also in education.**

> **Another reference to Le Corbusier, a figure ever central to the history of twentieth-century architecture, with his huge influence on very many architects of several generations, including Léon Stynen. A highly criticized figure, especially since the fiftieth anniversary of his death in 2015, among other things for his political views…**

Cependant il ne faut pas qu'il y ait confusion; le but de la construction n'a rien de commun avec celui de l'architecture. Je ne dis pas non plus que là où commence l'architecture cesse la construction, mais que celle-ci est la compagne généreuse et fidèle qui dès l'origine aide l'architecture à remplir les buts qu'elle s'est assignée, c'est à dire, répondre à des fonctions et donner à des intentions déterminées, une existence à la fois formelle et sensible.

On met en oeuvre de la pierre, du ciment, de l'acier, du bois; on en fait des maisons, des palais, des lieux de travail; c'est de la construction.

" Mais," nous dit Le Corbusier,"les murs s'élèvent sur le ciel dans un ordre tel que j'en suis ému. Je sens vos intentions. Vous étiez doux, brutal, charmant ou digne. Vos pierres me le disent. Vous m'attachez à cette place et mes yeux regardent; mes yeux regardent quelque chose qui énonce une pensée; une pensée qui s'éclaire sans mots ni sons, mais uniquement par des prismes qui ont entre eux des rapports. Ces prismes sont tels que la lumière les détaille clairement. Ces rapports n'ont trait à rien de nécessairement pratique ou descriptif. Ils sont une création mathématique de votre esprit. Ils sont le langage de l'architecture.

Obligations.
That is the term to which we must constantly make students attentive, but even more so ... critical! And we feel that these are becoming stricter and stricter, the mandatory rules that the architecture is required to take on board/exceed!

That is Léon Stynen *pur sang!* Strictness! Like his stationery, the way he tidied his desk... his architecture.

A very attractive, still highly relevant definition of architecture.

Ainsi, que de conditions doivent être remplies, pour que la forme née de servitudes innombrables acquière les qualités de l'éloquence, et que l'espace créé de mille formes devienne émouvant.

Là cependant est l'architecture, entité qui apparaît à la fois dans la rigueur technique de la construction, dans la valeur des formes et (dans) l'intelligence de l'espace.

L'espace n'est pas l'image négative de la forme comme c'est le cas pour la sculpture, mais il est le "creux" de l'architecture, le lieu où voyage le regard et s'accordent nos pensées.

Bien que délimité, soit par la forme interne, soit par les formes externes, l'espace fugitif, toujours changeant et surprenant, se rétrécit, se gonfle, se tend, apparaît, puis disparaît, suivant les mille et une perspectives que développe le modelé des formes.

C'est cet espace apparemment négligé qui, au delà des contingences matérielles, comprend toutes les tendances sentimentales, morales, ~~sociales~~ et intellectuelles.

Still topical. Once again topical. The fear of spatial experimentation that paralyses many architects often leads them to take refuge in a pseudo-polyvalent and pseudo-rational architectural and spatial neutrality, that both dispenses from and hampers essential debates about what architecture is and what it can offer.

Here perhaps an extra dimension to that advocated by his teacher Le Corbusier, for whom the plan, in a literal and figurative sense, was the essence of architecture – certainly in his early years.

Il est en fait le monde intérieur de l'architecture; il en est la plus grande richesse. C'est parce que les architectes actuels, (pour la plus grande part,) ignorent la valeur, sinon l'importance ~~l'existence même~~ de l'espace, que l'architecture courante d'aujourd'hui est si médiocre et vide de sens.

~~Or,~~ L'espace est l'essence même de l'architecture, mais il ne faudrait pas me faire dire ce que je ne veux pas dire, par exemple: que l'oeuvre architecturale n'existerait qu'en fonction exclusive de sa valeur spatiale - non - de nombreux facteurs interviennent en plus de ceux déjà cités. Chaque maison aussi modeste soit-elle, chaque édifice quelque soit son importance sont les résultats de l'application de programmes établis suivant une série d'éléments tels que: la qualité des individus, leur situation matérielle, leur style de vie, leurs coutumes, leurs rapports sociaux; les disciplines techniques et économiques; les aspirations, les croyances, les mythes enfin. Ce sont ces facteurs d'ordre humain, social, matériel et intellectuel qui dans la complexité de leurs rapports sont les éléments ordonnateurs des formes et de l'espace. C'est donc bien d'un tout qu'il s'agit comme je crois l'avoir dit déjà, mais, si dans la forme bâtie s'incrivent les signes tangibles de l'existence, c'est dans l'espace que rayonnent les raisons et les rêves.

Pour voir et comprendre une architecture, il faut donc préalablement reconnaître les qualités intérieures et extérieures de ses formes, sa valeur spatiale ainsi que l'exactitude de sa technique. Aussi pour saisir ces rapports est-il nécessaire de vivre l'architecture, la voir de ses yeux, la toucher de ses mains, y entendre sa voix; il est essentiel de se trouver " dedans " l'architecture; se la représenter par des dessins, des images, par la lecture ou l'information, ne suffit pas.

Dites-vous que je suis convaincu que tout ce que je pourrais dire en ce moment n'expliquera jamais le phénomène architectural.

J'insiste sur le fait que les meilleurs ouvrages dont je reconnais l'importance dans la formation artistique et la recherche, ces ouvrages, dis-je, même accompagnés de documents graphiques ou photographiques exceptionnels, n'apportent que peu de choses à la perception et à la révélation de l'architecture. A ce propos, j'aimerais vous raconter l'anecdote que voici:

This way of reading, judging and appreciating architecture is perhaps coloured by the architectural phenomenology inspired by Gaston Bachelard – for example in *La Poétique de l'espace* (1957) – and disseminated by, among others, Ernesto Nathan Rogers – a friend of Léon Stynen whom he met at the CIAMs – as editor-in-chief of the very important and influential Milanese magazine *Casabella Continuità*. That 'added soul' coupled with a more individual and 'corporeal' knowledge of architecture, which sought to recognize imagination, projections – including the users – poetry, etc., also resonates as the opposite of the abstract universalism of the first modern movement. There too we notice a strong evolution in Stynen.

Accompagnant une équipe de cinéastes professionnels en Inde pour réaliser un document sur Chandighar, capitale du Punjab, construite par Le Corbusier, j'avais tenté pendant le long voyage d'initier mes camarades à l'architecture et plus spécialement à celle que nous allions voir.

Le Corbusier m'avait remis une documentation très complète sur la ville ainsi que sur les principaux édifices.

Grâce à ces informations j'avais pu dégager les raisons qui avaient déterminé le tracé de la ville et celles qui avaient influencé la composition et l'ordonnance des constructions les plus représentatives: le Siège du Gouvernement, le Parlement, la Cour de Justice.

J'avais décrit, comme Le Corbusier me l'avait décrit: le site et l'habitat Indien.

Bref, après deux journées d'études mes camarades croyaient bien connaître Chandighar, son site et ses monuments, et il était entendu que le document cinématographique qu'ils allaient réaliser serait unique.

Après Delhi, deux heures de vol encore, et voici les plaines du Punjab, à l'horizon le Cachemir.

Chandighar est un immense espace vert découpé en de multiples zones; il y règne par le talent et l'intelligence d'un homme, la beauté, l'ordre et la paix.

La campagne environnante est nue. Dans le lointain, l'Himalaya dont les premiers sommets déjà se confondent avec le ciel.

De notre hôtel comme de toute la ville d'ailleurs, les édifices du Capitole sont invisibles; ils sont cachés par des collines venues là par le déversement de sables provenant des fouilles nécessaires à la construction. Le Corbusier en a dessiné les profils et les contours, créant un défilé que la nature n'aurait pu mieux faire. Un chemin y serpente paresseusement. Ce matin là, lorsque nous partîmes pour voir une des plus belles réalisations architecturales de l'époque, le soleil était haut déjà, la lumière était bleue, les ombres courtes et tranchantes, l'air léger; aucun bruit, aucune circulation sauf celle de quelques rickshaws, ces tricycles légers décorés de fleurs et de rubans. Nous étions joyeux et l'espace renvoyait l'écho de nos voix. Lorsque au détour du chemin, soudain, imprévisible, devant nous "l'architecture!"

Is it a coincidence that Léon Stynen visits the work of his 'teacher' Le Corbusier to support his thesis that architecture should be experienced? Moreover, this is a 'late' work, not of Le Corbusier's purism, but of his 'brutalist' period after the Cité radieuse, from which Stynen drew more or less direct inspiration in his projects of the 1960s – Harelbeke church, his family home on Lake Garda (1963)?

Quel événement! Quelle révélation!

Nous étions devenus silencieux, subjugués par la souveraine beauté de ces formes volontaires et douces à la fois, nues et blanches, soutenues par un jeu de couleurs dont l'alternance créait dans l'éclat de la lumière et le rythme des ombres comme des guirlandes de fleurs.

L'architecture était en fête et annonçait à ceux qui l'approchaient non seulement la dignité de l'existence humaine, mais encore celle de la liberté à laquelle tout un peuple s'était attaché.

Dois-je vous dire que nous étions fascinés par l'ampleur de l'espace dans lequel nous nous trouvions et d'où rayonnaient par la grâce de l'architecture, la Foi et l'Espérance d'une jeune nation.

Après.... longtemps après, mes compagnons rompant le silence me dirent: " Nous devrions remettre nos caméras dans nos bagages; jamais nous ne pourrons montrer "ça".

C'était vrai; ils avaient compris que ce qu'ils voulaient faire, ne serait jamais que le reflet d'un événement unique, d'une aventure exceptionnelle, qu'ils avaient eu le privilège de vivre et que l'architecture qu'ils comptaient emprisonner dans leur boîte à images, ne resterait jamais qu'imagé.

> A question – and not a statement – that still remains very open today.

Je m'excuse d'avoir ouvert cette parenthèse, mais j'ai pensé pouvoir mieux dire ainsi, que l'approche physique de l'architecture est la condition nécessaire pour en saisir la substance, en découvrir la signification et en réaliser le contenu.

Cependant ainsi que nous l'avons vu, bien des facteurs interviennent dans l'appréciation de l'architecture; et rechercher la signification d'une oeuvre bâtie, découvrir le contenu spatial d'un édifice, ou simplement s'expliquer une forme, demande autant de culture que de sensibilité. Mais vaut-il mieux approcher et juger l'architecture sous le signe de la connaissance que sous celui de l'intuition? Je ne sais; peut-être serait-il plus sage de ne juger les choses que lorsque l'élan du coeur rejoint la rigueur de la raison.

o o o o

Langage de l'architecture

Quand une oeuvre d'architecture est destinée à révéler une signification déterminée, celle-ci ne peut s'exprimer que par les rapports qui existent entre le fond et la forme visible, entre l'esprit et le signe.

— 15 —

> These issues may be less prominent today, now that the lifespan of buildings has become much shorter, but they will probably become more important again given the growing doubts about the demolition of buildings. Their fate and significance will become increasingly crucial.

Même mutilée, même défigurée par les hommes ou altérée par le temps, l'architecture porte en elle les sentiments et les intentions des individus ou des nations, quelles qu'aient été leur dépendance ou leur liberté.

L'architecture nous rapproche de la vie spirituelle des communautés disparues, elle traduit leurs aspirations, leurs angoisses.... leur effort idéaliste aussi; c'est pourquoi chaque époque, chaque style architectural est en réalité la révélation d'une métaphysique, la découverte d'impératifs mystérieux, le reflet d'une conscience, la reconnaissance d'un destin.

Il n'est pas inutile de dire que l'observance d'une morale s'exprime, non seulement dans le comportement journalier des individus ou dans la façon suivant laquelle s'organisent les sociétés, mais encore et surtout par le caractère du milieu physique créé de toutes pièces, ou plus exactement au travers des entités urbaines et rurales au coeur desquelles s'accomplit l'existence de chacun.

En parlant d'architecture, art collectif lequel dans toute civilisation apparaît le premier pour disparaître le premier, il est entendu que nous ne désignons pas uniquement les caractères et qualités plastiques des édifices, mais encore, ainsi que je viens de le dire, ceux de toutes les créations spatiales qui déterminent l'environnement et définissent le milieu.
L'architecture, en plus de ses qualités propres, a le privilège d'insérer dans ses espaces l'idéologie ou la morale d'individus ou de groupes agissant suivant certains principes.

Moins définies que les documents écrits, puisque, c'est de symboles qu'il s'agit, les pierres nous renseignent sur les qualités spirituelles d'une société, et lorsque tout signe d'écriture a disparu, elles nous permettent encore de saisir la vie intérieure de ceux qui par elles ont voulu exprimer leurs tendances les plus profondes et les plus vraies: " ces instants de la pensée dans la matière impérissable" comme l'a si bien dit Louis Hourticq.

Il ne faudrait pas penser cependant que je sous-estime la valeur des textes et l'importance inestimable de leur apport, mais j'insiste, les édifices nous parlent autant que les écrits et c'est grâce à eux que nous pouvons faire la synthèse d'une civilisation, même si les inscriptions qui les accompagnent sont effacées, même si le sens de ces inscriptions reste secret.

" Civilisation. " Peut-être n'est-il pas superflu de rappeler que la civilisation est l'ensemble des caractères inhérents à la morale, à la vie intellectuelle, artistique et matérielle d'un peuple, et non, ainsi que beaucoup le supposent, uniquement la somme des conditions propres à l'expansion technique et sociale d'une nation.
A vrai dire, il ne saurait être question de civilisation tant que n'apparaît pas l'ambition d'atteindre les sources de la sensibilité, de cette sensibilité d'où naît le besoin qu'éprouve l'homme de communier avec l'esprit universel et qui est la condition même de son épanouissement.

> Ainsi connaître et comprendre l'architecture nous rapproche de l'intelligence de l'homme et de l'Univers. Depuis toujours des peuples ont su exprimer leurs croyances, leur puissance, leurs idéaux, leurs besoins les plus profonds, en bâtissant des édifices qui aujourd'hui encore, nous racontent leur merveilleuse ou tragique aventure.

What examples, what history?
Following his predilection for ahistorical architecture, Stynen here resorts to classical architectural history – Egypt / Persia / Greece / Ancient Rome / Byzantium / Islam / Romanesque / Gothic / Renaissance / Baroque / Classicism – to build his credo. Everything serves the proposition that architecture illustrates the state in which a society finds itself, and that high-quality architecture matches a moral society.

Exemples historiques

• L'Egypte •

An equivalence that we now know to be a pure construction and totally theoretical. Moreover, this Eurocentric history itself is highly controversial, a major problem area also in all architecture schools, partly due to the professionalization – also historical – of research into architecture and the significance it has acquired. All this under the influence of gender studies, the rereading of history, post-colonial studies etc.

> Ainsi l'Egypte, qui par l'énorme durée et la puissance soutenue de son effort, constitue la plus grande civilisation qui ait paru sur terre, a-t-elle attesté de son idéal "par" l'architecture; durant plus de 5.000 ans elle restera plongée dans l'architecture, et qui plus est, fidèle à une conception architecturale infrangible de l'Univers.
>
> Dans des monuments d'une impressionante beauté elle ne cessera d'inscrire la peur d'un sommeil sans lendemain et l'espoir d'un lointain retour. Emprisonnés par le désert, sur les rives du grand fleuve qui rythme leur vie, les Egyptiens qu'Hérodote définissait " les plus religieux de tous les hommes", ont bâti pour leurs dieux des temples et pour leurs rois des tombeaux à l'échelle de leurs croyances et de leurs traditions.

> Dans l'espace de leurs édifices les plus prestigieux, dans leurs sculptures monumentales, dans l'alignement et le style des signes hiéroglyphiques, transparaient une intangible rigueur morale et la reconnaissance d'une étonnante et divine autorité.
>
> Le Sacré s'inscrit en avant d'immenses solitudes et le temple est aussi fermé au monde extérieur que replié sur son contenu spirituel. Que de rites mystérieux annoncent ces cortèges de sphinx et quelle implacable volonté expriment ces pylones qui <u>marquent l'interdit des espaces initiatiques</u>. Passé le seuil exorciste, se succèdent péristyles, cours intérieures et salles hypostyles, rythmés à la cadence des nombres secrets. Chaque pierre alors dira les raisons de vivre ou racontera ce que sera l'ultime voyage.
>
> L'architecture ici s'est appropriée la sculpture et les formes nées de leur accord ont acquis le privilège surnaturel de dialoguer avec le soleil; sur elles glissent les ombres et apparaissent les intentions, les angoisses, les promesses et les espérances d'une nation.

Annotations:

- And of much disgraceful behaviour, exploitations, various kinds of immorality, etc., which were not discussed at that time… not yet.
- Pure poetry, and transcendentalism in a way.

Cependant, je m'en voudrais de ne pas souligner l'âme poétique de ce peuple, son charme et sa douceur, qualités qui se retrouvent non seulement dans la peinture et la sculpture, mais encore dans certains temples. (Philae, par exemple,) dont la grâce et les proportions rappellent que les Egyptiens furent aussi les initiateurs des grecs.

. La Perse.

L'architecture de la civilisation mésopotamienne, faite d'argile et enfouie dans les sables, ayant laissé peu de vestiges, tout de suite après l'Egypte je vous parlerai des Perses, ce peuple d'origine nomade descendu des Hauts Plateaux de l'Iran et qui devait créer le plus grand empire du monde antique.

Par des inscriptions patiemment déchiffrées nous savons que ces conquérants pratiquaient l'occultisme et le culte de Mithra, qu'ils avaient le sens de l'humain et de l'équité. Tolérants et probes, ils laissèrent vivre de leur vie traditionnelle

We notice in Léon Stynen a fascination for a civilization with which he feels philosophically related, a fascination that makes this society more perfect for him than it perhaps was and thus colours his architectural judgement, because based on moral values.

les régions que leur étaient soumises et respectèrent leurs dieux. Grâce aux souverains perses le monde antique ne connut plus qu'exceptionnellement l'intolérance religieuse.

" J'ai aimé la justice et j'ai haï le mensonge," dit Darius. " Ma volonté a été qu'aucune injustice ne soit faite à la veuve et à l'orphelin; j'ai strictement puni le menteur mais celui qui labourait je l'ai récompensé."

Mais c'est dans l'austérité de son architecture que se révèle le plus clairement la grandeur de cette nation dont la puissance s'exprime non ~~pas~~ par des temples puisque les autels suffisaient à ses divinités, mais par d'immenses palais. Chaque souverain à son tour exige le sien et le sentiment exalté de la royauté fait que l'architecture, devenue art royal, magnifie à la fois la monarchie, la dynastie et le roi, chef religieux, politique et militaire.

Ruines grandioses d'un passé fabuleux, les palais de Persépolis dont la disposition rappelle la tradition nomade, dressent sur un plateau rocheux la majesté de leur architecture qu'adoucit la grâce alors naissante de l'Ionie.... Sur les parois qui limitent les escaliers géants, des sculptures monumentales louent les mérites et les exploits du souverain avec une netteté et une fréquence insistantes.

Inlassablement célébrés, le roi, toujours le roi, ses sujets, ses soldats, ses victoires.... une litanie de pierre itérative obsédante comme une incantation.
" Persépolis, écrit Louis Hourticq, " est l'oeuvre dernière des civilisations antiques, le monument suprême, le testament de la vieille Asie."
Les tombeaux taillés en croix dans la haute roche abrupte ont des façades de palais, toujours et encore des palais, que soutiennent et surmontent d'énormes sculptures en relief, rythmées à la mesure d'un lent et solennel cortège.
Aujourd'hui palais et tombeaux menacés d'érosion restent l'ultime message d'une morale originelle basée sur la fidélité d'homme à homme, c'est-à-dire sur l'ascendant du chef, ascendant mérité par son courage et sa droiture, par son amour de la justice et son mépris du mensonge.

Mais à ces civilisations impériales qui ont uniquement pour fin l'Etat personnifié par un roi - être surhumain souvent divinisé - s'oppose peu à peu "l'humanisme" des peuples qui forment dans le Proche Orient des groupements restreints et occupent de petits territoires. Ainsi les états égéens, phénicien, araméen.... Israël, dont le rôle dans l'histoire de l'humanité sera considérable.

La Grèce.

Alors la puissante, la redoutable armée de l'immense empire Perse fut tenue en échec par une nation cent fois plus petite en population et en étendue, une nation pauvre et courageuse: la Grèce. Terre ingrate mais souriante, saturée de lumière, une mer heureuse.... là, malgré les invasions se forma une triple unité de langue, de culture et de religion, là se manifesta la pensée libre qui devait engager l'univers dans une phase décisive.

L'histoire de la Grèce, pays de contraste, où l'ombre s'oppose avec intensité à la lumière, a aussi ses côtés sombres et ses pages noires, mais ni les errements, ni le scandale de l'esclavage ne purent ternir ce qu'il y avait en elle d'ouvert et de généreux.

Nous n'ignorons pas que c'est à l'esprit critique des anciens Grecs, à leur sentiment de la liberté et à leur amour de la vérité que nous devons d'être devenus ce que nous sommes.

Un passé agité, des excès et des rivalités n'empêcheront ni la cohésion, ni l'unité morale d'un peuple pour qui l'idéal ne cessera d'être celui de la perfection éthique, idéal qui demeurera fixé à jamais dans son architecture.

Le Parthénon incarne ce moment unique, ce moment de grâce et de plénitude. Dans sa lumineuse et émouvante beauté il est l'image sensible de la pensée grecque, qui pendant 25 siècles influencera l'histoire humaine.

Ses colonnes aux lignes volontaires et pures, le langage des métopes et le rythme des triglyphes, le tracé et le volume des frontons, leurs saillies de lumière et leurs creux d'ombre, révèlent une tension vers un équilibre parfait, un désir éperdu de se surpasser, la recherche passionnée d'un absolu.

On dit du Parthénon qu'il est rigoureux comme un théorème, mais " l'élan des colonnes obliques, dit Elie Faure, la courbe insensible qui arrondit l'architrave, tous ces écarts imperceptibles, animent le temple et lui donnent le battement d'un coeur."

Si le principe du temple grec est toujours le même, ses proportions indéfiniment pareilles, toujours la loi du nombre le met à l'échelle du monde spirituel et matériel dont il est le résumé. Cependant ni l'impérieuse domination du style, ni l'asservissement à la formule du rectangle à double fronton ne paralysent, ni stérilisent l'esprit de l'architecte, au contraire, écoutons Eupalinos s'exprimant dans l'oeuvre de Paul Valéry:

" Ce petit temple que j'ai bâti pour Hermès
à quelques pas d'ici, si tu savais ce qu'il
est pour moi! Où le passant ne voit qu'une
élégante chapelle, c'est peu de chose: quatre
colonnes, un style très simple, j'ai mis le
souvenir d'un clair jour de ma vie.
O douce métamorphose! Ce temple délicat, nul
ne le sait, est l'image mathématique d'une fille
de Corinthe que j'ai heureusement aimée. Il en
reproduit fidèlement les proportions particulières.
Il vit pour moi, il me rend ce que je lui ai donné."

Comment serait-il possible d'expliquer mieux le langage de l'architecture et son contenu spirituel.

La Rome antique.

Quand Rome étendit son empire jusqu'aux confins de l'Occident, que ses légions se répandirent dans le Proche Orient et le Nord de l'Afrique, le monde peu à peu se transforma.

Si l'empire romain s'était contenté d'en imposer par la force, son règne aurait été éphémère mais recevant, donnant et transformant, il devait, grâce à son génie organisateur, devenir le centre d'une civilisation dont l'unité politique et militaire ne cessa d'être étayée par les progrès d'une unité économique et morale.

Capitale d'un monde, Rome n'a pas seulement été à l'origine d'une civilisation, elle a su aussi préserver une part importante de l'héritage grec et permis à l'Hellénisme de pénétrer en Occident. A elle revient d'avoir égalisé la situation juridique de tous les hommes libres, d'avoir créé la "virtus" latine, c.à.d. la solidité et la sensibilité propres au monde latin.

L'âme complexe du romain, mélange de spiritualité et de sensualité, de simplicité et d'orgueil, se révèle dans des oeuvres dont l'ampleur force le respect: ainsi les thermes, les arènes, les basiliques.... temoins d'un des moments les plus décisifs de l'histoire de l'humanité.
Par ailleurs, lorsqu'il s'agit d'oeuvres purement utilitaires le romain dit des choses étonnantes: ses routes, ses ponts et ses acqueducs géants, manifestations pétrifiées de son implacable volonté d'organiser et de planifier le monde.

Mais la puissance et l'unité de Rome, sa force et sa lucidité sont traduites le plus éloquemment par le Panthéon, édifice remarquable dont la beauté se révèle dans l'audace d'une technique magistrale et dans l'admirable fréquence harmonique des formés, celle des caissons de la coupole en particulier.

La clarté qui tombe de l'ouverture laissée libre dans le dôme et où certains ne voient qu'une prise de lumière, n'est-elle pas le symbole du rayonnement de Rome, de Rome où a commencé notre civilisation et qui en a assuré la pérennité au travers des siècles de barbarie? Le Panthéon pour qui veut lire l'architecture est le message le plus concis et le plus émouvant que nous ait laissé l'Empire romain.

• Byzance •

Lorsque Byzance prit la relève, le temporel s'unit au spirituel et à l'impérial se substitua le sacré. Héritier de la civilisation héllénique, de l'empire romain et de la religion orthodoxe, l'empire byzantin durant mille ans resta debout.

Alors l'architecture créa son monde, un des plus beaux et des plus authentiques qui soient, un monde fermé, éclairé de l'intérieur dont l'espace semble se dilater et se projeter au dehors; " espace où s'impose, dit Elie Faure, la mystérieuse présence du nombre."
Les églises byzantines révèlent l'existence, (au moins chez les élites), d'une culture raffinée, d'une vie intime intense et notamment de ce sentiment si rare: une piété infinie.

Malgré un riche essor intellectuel, Byzance resta
fermée aux influences étrangères et vécut repliée
sur elle même. Cet univers clos explique l'indifférence
de l'architecture byzantine à tout effort de beauté
extérieure. Faite d'immatérialité et d'infini
~~elle~~ l'architecture ici fait corps avec la décoration intérieure, avec
le marbre dont sont revêtues les colonnes, avec
le porphyre des pavements, le coloris des fresques,
la dentelle des chapiteaux ajourés, mais surtout
avec la mosaïque dont l'éclat précieux en épouse
la forme initiale, en exprime la substance,
" en partage et totalise la dignité."

      Ainsi dans le Mausolée de Galla Placidia,
à Ravennes, par exemple, la mosaïque qui fait chanter
ses bleus profonds se confond avec l'architecture
et lui donne suivant l'expression d'Henri Van Lier:
" la transparence dorée de l'au-delà."

. L'Islam .

      L'essor de l'Islam, né des espaces
infinis et des étendues désertiques par la volonté
d'un seul homme, a l'apparence d'un prodige. Quand les
chevaliers du prophète entreprirent leurs conquêtes,
animés d'un immense élan de foi, ils parvinrent à
créer partout un monde à eux tout en restant ouverts
au génie des peuples vaincus.

" Un peuple fanatique, errant, " a écrit Guy de Maupassant, " à peine capable de construire des murs, venu sur une terre couverte de ruines laissées par ses prédécesseurs, il y ramassa partout ce qui lui parut de plus beau, et, à son tour avec ces débris de même style et de même ordre, éleva, mû par une inspiration sublime une demeure à son dieu, faite de morceaux arrachés aux villes croulantes, mais aussi parfaite que les plus pures conceptions des plus grands tailleurs de pierre."

Dans les mosquées il semble que l'espace puisse s'étendre, se prolonger toujours plus avant et les colonnes se multiplier à l'infini, créant un monde illimité, sans commencement ni fin, à l'image de l'irrésistible et progressive expansion de la pensée arabe. Au Maghreb et en Asie Centrale l'architecture a la majesté qu'évoque le désert: Kairouan.... En Espagne elle se pare de grâce et de facile séduction: l'Alhambra de Grenade.... En Turquie elle rayonne de poésie et de vie intérieure intense: la mosquée bleue à Istambul.... En Inde elle a la précision et les délicatesses d'un joyau: le Taj Mahal.... en Iran elle est enluminée comme une miniature: Ispahan....

> We also feel here a special 'tenderness' in Léon Stynen, who idealized this medieval society with its brotherhoods and its lodges, this organization, this sense of duty, this humility ... all values that are even more dear to him because (see *infra*) he sees them disappearing from society at that 'end' of the twentieth century, of which he is a part.

Je pense aussi à l'architecture révélatrice des grands caravansérails aujourd'hui silencieux; ces lieux magiques où flottent les souvenirs de lointains départs et qui connurent les déchirements et les espoirs ~~d'un peuple.~~ *le tant d'hommes liés au même destin.*

Le Roman

L'an mil apparaît en Occident comme une brillante aurore. En même temps que l'épanouissement de l'Europe féodale, commença alors la grande aventure romane.

A tous les carrefours de la Chrétienté et sur les longues routes des pélerinages, la construction s'organisa " suivant une métrique," dit Bruno Zévi, " parallèle à la métrique intentionnelle et poétique." Les architectes-maçons, les tailleurs de pierre, les charpentiers et les imagiers unirent leurs efforts dans un fraternel coude à coude et oeuvrèrent de toute leur âme et de tout leur coeur à l'édification de leurs chapelles, abbayes ou églises.

Réunis en loges, ils parlent le même langage, acceptent les mêmes devoirs et vivent du même espoir. Tous connaissent la charité et, *j'insiste*, chacun a l'humilité de demeurer à son rang. Aussi n'est-il pas exagéré de dire que si dans leur travail ils étaient fidèles à l'esprit de compagnonnage, c'est qu'il en était de même dans leur vie de tous les jours. Leurs oeuvres furent parfois imparfaites, n'importe, elles restent le témoignage de la miraculeuse intensité d'invention qui se manifesta alors dans toute la civilisation occidentale.

Avec ses pleins cintres et ses piliers trapus, l'architecture romane, architecture dépouillée, atteint par le seul équilibre des masses nues à la plus pure et à la plus émouvante beauté.
Née d'un idéal commun de coöpération et d'entr'aide, elle est à la fois une profonde manifestation d'humilité et de conviction religieuse et, quelle qu'ait été sa dépendance dogmatique, l'expression d'une pensée particulièrement élevée.

Le Gothique.

Au XIe siècle, quand l'unité de l'Eglise se sentit menacée, une ère nouvelle s'annonça pour l'Occident chrétien, ère d'organisation et de discipline, d'unité et d'équilibre. A ce moment le plein cintre se brisa et le Gothique, appelé aussi art français, commença sa prodigieuse et exaltante ascension.

La pierre alors perd sa pesanteur et se dématérialise, les piliers jaillissent, les arcs se croisent et l'espace magnifie la foi chrétienne, mais une foi plus humaine et plus réaliste, plus calculée et passionnée aussi que celle qui marqua l'époque romane. La cathédrale deviendra l'arme subtile, l'argument pénétrant dont l'Eglise usera pour lutter contre l'évolution des idées et le progrès de l'esprit laïc.

Lieu d'incantation plus que de prière, lieu magique où se déroulent les "mystères" et les fêtes, maison de l'absolu, astucieusement placée sous le signe de la Vierge au sourire tendre, elle accueille confréries et corporations en de solennelles processions.

Si les abbatiales et églises romanes sont l'oeuvre de moines, les cathédrales gothiques et les constructions civiles sont les réalisations des Communes, ces entités vaillantes autant que généreuses, souvent impatientes, souvent révoltées lesquelles, dit Henri Van Lier " n'avaient qu'une âme jusqu'en leur dernier recoin, grâce à l'homogénéité de leur style et à une entente de mitoyenneté où les maisons s'accolaient et se chevauchaient en des empiétements fraternels."

Ce fut le grand moment de l'Europe féodale, moment de force, de noblesse et de courage. Les châteaux nous le disent. Ce fut aussi le temps de la recherche et de la plus folle témérité. Beauvais en est la preuve: cathédrale gigantesque deux fois effondrée et deux fois reconstruite sous le signe des mêmes convictions, des mêmes contestations et d'un même courage.

Ainsi en ce XIV siècle, quand vint le crépuscule du Moyen-Age, Nicolas d'Autrecourt pouvait professer enfin: " Rien ne m'autorise d'affirmer qu'il y ait autre chose que ce qui vient de mes cinq sens et de mes expérimentations." Principe <u>scientifique</u> s'il en est.

De même devaient penser ceux qui, malgré la crainte de Dieu et au-delà de la prière, firent tenir debout les cathédrales.

. La Renaissance .

Puis la Chrétienté vit se craqueler de toutes parts l'univers étroit mais quasi invulnérable qui avait été le sien, les conquêtes de la mer et les découvertes du ciel, l'invention de l'imprimerie, " ces foudroyantes lumières" dont parle Michelet, donnèrent au monde d'autres dimensions et chacun le contempla avec des yeux neufs et une sensibilité autre.

Ce fut le début d'une période exaltante " le clair matin de la Renaissance", l'art et le savoir se renouvelèrent, la forme traditionnelle de la pensée se transforma, l'individualisme s'affirma dans tous les domaines et l'homme devenu le centre de la création s'imagina être "unique" en même temps qu'universel.

Pic de la Mirandole prête à Dieu ces paroles adressées à Adam dans la légende de la création et qui pourraient être écrites en exergue d'une histoire de la Renaissance: " Je t'ai placé au centre du monde pour mieux voir ce qui s'y passe. Tu n'es ni divin ni terrestre, mortel ou immortel, si bien que comme ton propre créateur tu peux te façonner comme tu le désires. Tu as le pouvoir de sombrer au niveau des brutes ou celui de renaître dans un ordre plus élevé et plus noble, suivant ton propre jugement."

L'architecture alors devint le reflet de ce monde nouveau, de ce sentiment jeune et libre qui réclamait de l'homme un effort constant vers une plus haute perfection.
L'équilibre rigoureux des plans et le rythme sévère des façades sont adoucis par l'atmosphère de joie et d'évasion qui rayonne des vastes cours intérieures et dispense à ces palais merveilleux une grâce et une transparence reflétant l'idéal de vie, l'ouverture d'esprit et la liberté de pensée de ceux qui y vivaient. Je pense au palais des Ducs d'Urbino, non loin d'Assise, où des décors d'inspiration paienne voisinent avec d'autres qui enferment la plus haute spiritualité.

Le passage de l'expression communautaire à l'expression individuelle changea le visage des villes, l'édifice privé prit le pas sur l'édifice collectif, l'édifice civil sur l'édifice religieux: les lieux du culte sont davantage des palais que des églises. Partout se retrouve la domination de l'homme tout puissant, supérieur à tous et à tout, de l'homme créateur et vainqueur qui a trouvé en sa triple aspiration vers le beau, le bien et le vrai le secret de son épanouissement.
Voilà, je crois ce que révèle l'architecture sur les valeurs spirituelles de l'élite à l'époque de la Renaissance.

. Le Baroque .

Beaucoup soutiennent que le brillant mais bref éclat de la Renaissance fut effacé par l'influence de la Contre-Réforme, c'est-à-dire, par le renouveau du Catholicisme qui marque le début de la période baroque. La question est bien plus complexe: c'est en réalité un vaste mouvement d'évasion qui se retrouve dans les arts comme dans la mystique et la politique du temps.

After trying to convince us of the overriding importance of experience – see his visit to Chandigarh – it may seem paradoxical that he uses nothing more – or nothing less – than abstract moral value as a yardstick for societies and the architecture that 'reflects' them. And it is not 'surprising' that the baroque is associated with the period that most closely resembles the one in which he evolves and lives and which he considers ... amoral.

Le Baroque peut être considéré comme une constante historique, élément permanent qui se retrouve à certaines périodes et qui intéresse toute la civilisation. " Phénomène," dit Eugenio d'Ors, " qui rappelle à certaines sociétés, lasses de raffinement et de rationalité, les symboles élémentaires, fils de l'instinct."

Ainsi la période baroque pourrait dans une certaine mesure être rapprochée de la nôtre. En effet, en ce XVII siècle comme aujourd'hui, les sociétés semblent se laisser aller à l'anarchie et à la dissolution, tout n'est que trouble et chaos, contradiction aussi.
Alors que naît la plus grande floraison de saints que l'Eglise ait jamais connue: Jean de la Croix, Thérèse, Xavier, Ignace, pour ne nommer que ceux-là, les "libertins" prônent la volupté et une morale de plaisirs. Au Théâtre on viole sur scène et l'inceste s'étale avec complaisance.

L'architecture révèle cette contradiction métaphysique et ces oppositions, elle traduit l'angoisse de l'homme en proie à ses incertitudes, en même temps que sa volonté de retrouver à la fois les sources profondes de l'Univers et les valeurs humaines fondamentales.

Le Baroque prétend à la surprise et à l'étonnement, il rompt les frontons, tord les colonnes, multiplie les volutes, les formes se détruisent et se recomposent suivant le mouvement même de la vie, et ce dynamisme est encore accentué par la peinture spatiale où le Seigneur triomphant au milieu de saintes femmes sensuelles semble se mouvoir dans l'infini des désirs accordés.

Parti d'Italie, l'art baroque passera mers et océans et gagnera tous les pays Catholiques. En Amérique du Sud, les Jésuites se serviront de sa prodigieuse exubérance décorative pour impressionner les fidèles et utiliseront le côté scénique de l'architecture pour mettre en valeur la doctrine et les mystères du dogme.

. Le Classicisme .

Toujours au XVIIe siècle le centre de gravité de la culture occidentale se déplace vers la France qui jouit alors, malgré les guerres nombreuses, d'une stabilité relative. C'est ainsi qu'en marge du Baroque et par réaction contre la diversité, la dispersion et la licence, naîtra le Classicisme, issu de traditions et d'une morale autres.

La personne humaine se dégage et s'affirme, les tendances bourgeoises et celles de la noblesse d'épée commencent à s'équilibrer; le XVIIe est le siècle de l'épanouissement spirituel et du progrès de la science, celui de Pascal et de Descartes, celui aussi où l'esthétique veut s'appuyer sur l'éthique et la logique.

Le temps des communes rebelles et des factions religieuses étant révolu, le souci de l'indépendance et de la grandeur nationale fait du roi, héros souverain, le symbole de la monarchie absolue, l'image même de Dieu. Or cette monarchie demandait une architecture théatrale susceptible d'étonner le peuple tout en le flattant; Versailles, par exemple, est le décor où se déroula le spectacle prestigieux de la royauté toute puissante. L'architecture, libre de toute altération émotionnelle, est solennelle et cadencée comme una pavane de Lulli; les façades du palais s'étirent avec autorité devant les salles immenses qui retenaient prisonnière une noblesse soumise et fascinée.

Architecture aussi les jardins en terrasses que joignent les escaliers monumentaux, les miroirs d'eau qu'irise le jaillissement des fontaines, la géométrie des murs de feuillage et les théâtres de verdure où le roi, déguisé en dieu de l'Olympe, se jouait son propre personnage.

Epris de rigueur et de logique, le Classicisme tend à réaliser une unité de totalité et sa recherche de l'universel s'exprime par un constant souci de perfection.

Le besoin d'ordre autant que de raison du Classicisme s'affirme non seulement dans les châteaux mais aussi dans les villes par de grandes compositions symétriques; les places sont axées et les avenues s'alignent suivant l'esprit d'une société encadrée et hiërarchisée. Plus tard s'établira l'usage de vivre " de façon civile entre bâtiments." Comment ne pas penser à la place de la Carrière à Nancy, à son architecture noble et harmonieuse où se devine si bien la culture et l'urbanité de la société d'alors.

Avant de se déssécher en néo-classicisme, l'architecture se nuancera de fluidité et de grâce, derrière des façades moins sévères surgiront des décors charmants, ceux des salons ou des cénacles qui avaient été le noyau de l'Académie Française et que la Révolution devait disperser.

Conclusion - notre temps

Ainsi ayant remonté le temps, ai-je voulu démontrer combien sont accordées les valeurs spirituelles et morales d'une société et l'architecture, combien subtil est son pouvoir poétique et grand son éloquence.... alors que diront les ruines de nos édifices? Qu'évoqueront les traces de nos villes?

Certes notre civilisation n'est pas comme les autres et si Malraux a pu dire qu'elle n'a su construire ni un temple ni un tombeau, Emmanuel Berl répond avec pertinence que " le bizarre n'est pas l'impuissance de notre civilisation à construire un temple et un tombeau, mais bien qu'elle applaudisse quand on le lui reproche.

Because this text is a kind of testament, Stynen cannot avoid looking at 'his' society in which he moves. And which he judges very negatively ... especially its architecture.

Just like Le Corbusier fifty years earlier in his 'Rappels à MM. les architectes' in *Vers une architecture,* he seems to emphasize that architecture and architects are not up to the level as the society in which they operate. Is it a – bad – passing moment? Civilization produces extraordinary things, the examples speak for themselves – from IBM to NASA to Sputnik, while in 1923 Le Corbusier was talking about airplanes and passenger ships… Its references are also technological, captivating and reflecting a society that has certainly produced miracles, but which has not – yet – found its full architectural expression.

Même le cercueil de Lénine fait mesquin à côté de la pyramide de Chéops, mais Chéops n'avait pas de spoutnik et si Houston n'a pas son Parthénon, Athènes n'avait pas sa N.A.S.A. On ne peut pas tout faire l'Erechteion et l'I.B.M."

Et cependant notre civilisation qui accumule les prodiges s'enlise dans les sables ou se perd dans les labyrinthes dont elle ne voit comment sortir. Salomon demandait à Dieu la sagesse mais les hommes, en général, préfèrent la folie et la contradiction. La vie actuelle ne se sépare-t-elle pas de la vie, et l'homme d'aujourd'hui ne se complait-il pas dans l'artificiel et l'illusion.

Very harsh judgments about Western society in the early 1970s and – what foreknowledge – an almost pre-ecological way of thinking, a sensitivity to the limits of the system – which he embodies in a way.

Particularly heavy outbursts against the society of his time.

Que l'espèce humaine se multiplie inconsidérément, qu'elle contamine ce qui l'entoure est un fait, mais était-il nécessaire de déclarer la guerre à la nature et sommes-nous certains de trouver le bonheur dans un monde technologique sinon mécanisé....?

Déjà s'élève la voix des contestataires, ces citoyens de sociétés en devenir qui proclament à leur façon que le monde dans sa forme présente est pourri et sans rédemption possible.

Il est vrai que nous vivons dans une impureté morale qui dépasse l'imagination: les pouvoirs politiques sont viciés jusqu'à la moelle - le scandale est partout parce que la décision n'est nulle part. Très éloignée de la démocratie la société agit dans la licence, la vénalité, la compromission et l'abus. Nos milieux urbains, nos lieux de travail n'en sont-ils pas la dramatique image, et jamais peut-être, l'architecture a été plus éloquente pour exprimer les abandons d'une société sans principes.

Il y a 25 ans déjà je donnais à entendre que les sociétés vivent dans le milieu urbain qu'elles méritent.

'Opening the eyes' remains a reference to Le Corbusier – almost a quote – (see supra).

Just like Gropius, Le Corbusier and others in the early twentieth century, Stynen reveals his fascination with technological achievements, for him the only advances that can formally and morally compete with the great achievements of the past.

Dans ce cas il ne reste qu'à ouvrir les yeux pour savoir ce que vaut la nôtre.
Tel est le côté sombre de l'architecture d'aujourd'hui, reste le côté clair, celui de nos recherches et de nos espérances.

Au début de cette conférence je disais: " qu'en parlant d'architecture, je n'entendais pas uniquement le caractère des édifices de nature traditionnelle, mais celui de toutes les créations spatiales qui déterminent un milieu.
Ainsi sont architecture aussi, les hauts lieux de la technologie, fruits de la science: les barrages, les centrales hydro-électriques, les ponts qui traversent rivières et bras de mer, les espaces où se construisent les fusées interplanétaires, ces ateliers gigantesques plus vastes que nos cathédrales; toutes constructions à la mesure du siècle et qui rendent à l'architecture sa vraie substance.

Ainsi la dualité qui existe dans le domaine de l'expression architecturale: d'une part la laideur des villes et des régions, d'autre part la beauté *fondamentale* ~~et la logique~~ de quelques édifices choisis, est-elle la preuve de nos débordements comme aussi de notre saine raison.

He ends with a very abstract, very short and very little argued/illustrated note, which does offer a hint of hope.

He wants to preserve reasons to believe in and hope for a world, an architecture based on the trio of morality/wisdom/strength… without forgetting beauty! A whole programme that is still very relevant in the practice and teaching of architecture.

Mais viendra le jour de la synthèse; déjà s'inscrivent dans certains tracés, dans de rares espaces ou dans quelques formes construites, les messages d'hommes isolés, lucides, courageux et droits, qui ont su garder la foi en un monde plus juste et plus humain.

Si comme eux nous ne perdons pas l'espoir et cherchons à réaliser, dans la mesure de nos moyens, un équilibre entre les forces contradictoires qui bousculent notre société, alors naîtra, peut être, une architecture qui rayonnera dans l'histoire à l'honneur de notre monde: une architecture faite de Sagesse, de Force et de Beauté.

Léon STYNEN

Anvers, le 13/11/1972
Mons, le 10/ 5/1973

FORMS & FUNCTIONS

LUC VINCENT

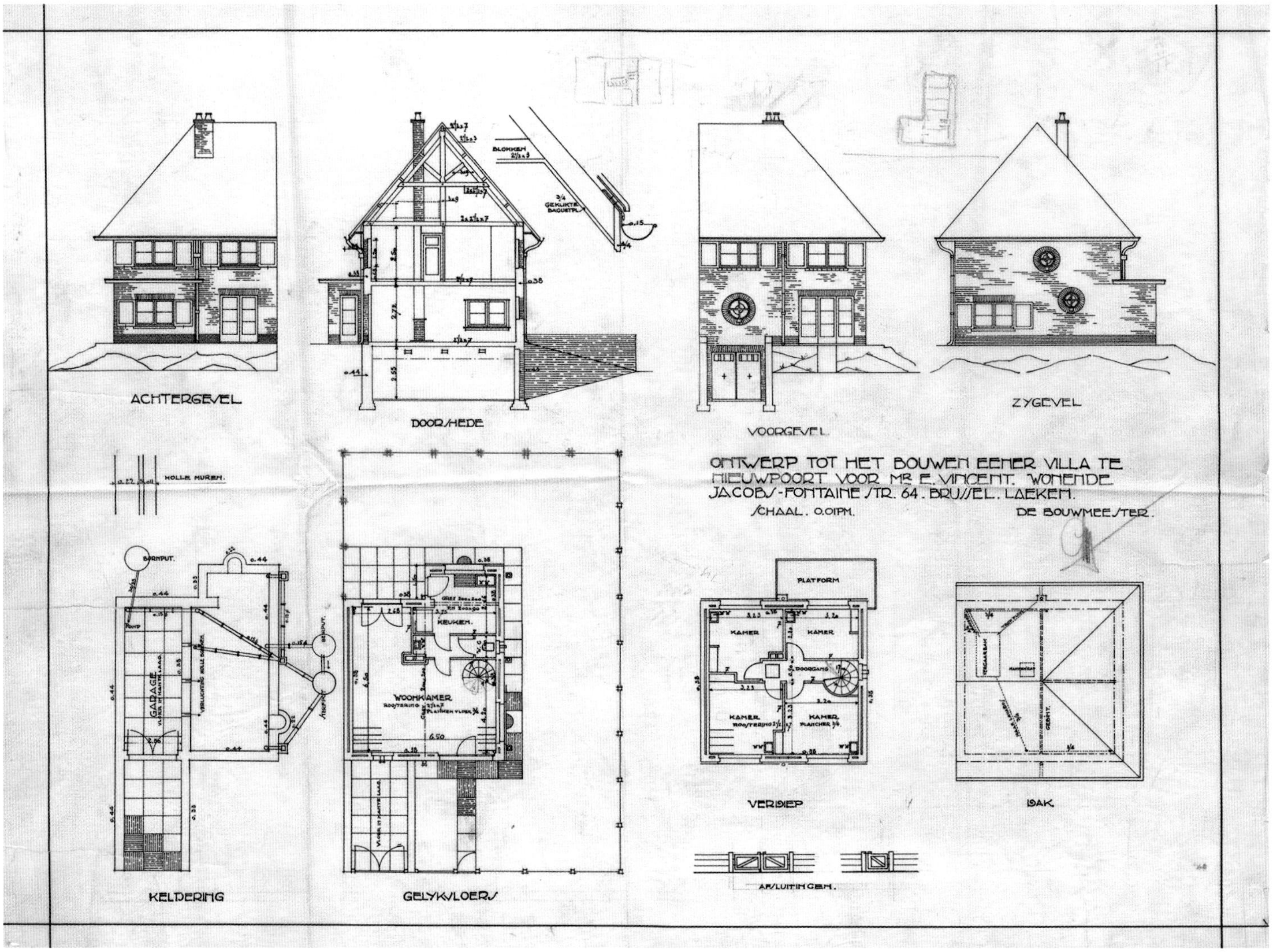

Holiday home, Nieuwpoort, 1930-31

Here is the introduction to the Wikipedia entry (in French) on Léon Stynen:[1]
Léon Stynen is a Belgian architect who took part in the Art Deco movement during the 1920s, the modernist movement during the 1930s and the functionalist movement during the 1950s.

Listing architects, designers and artists according to theoretical standards and without nuance is over-simplistic. We will endeavour to perceive in Stynen the traces he left in the history of furniture, and of Belgian design.

The first pieces appear in his studies for the furniture of a private house in Nieuwpoort.

1 Accessed December 2022.

As was customary at that time, the architect also designed the few main pieces of furniture. Of simple design, these were produced by local craftsmen, usually in wood. We are a long way from post-war industrialization.

The shapes are obviously functionalist, with, for the two low chairs, a touch of 'romanticism'. From there to qualifying them as 'Art Deco' is for us one step too far. In them we see rather a concern for quality and attention paid to proportions and to the joinery, a know-how based on a way of life. We can't talk about design here either. No… we are what is intimate and what is feasible for a craftsman.

The naturalness of the chair is comparable to that of the furniture that Léon Stynen designed for the Kursaal in Ostend. This is due to the wood and the traditional craft methods used.

The furniture, produced by the woodworking school of the Royal Atheneum Emile Bockstael in Laeken, exudes a form of classicism deriving from the craftsman's tools.

In harmony with the architecture, which is itself of an order that also expresses a positive humanism.

Léon Stynen created three casinos, each of which left its mark on 1950s Belgium. With their strong, modernist identities, Chaudfontaine, Knokke and Ostend are places of timeless presence.

The Ostend Kursaal is a large complex extending over more than one hectare. For this project, Léon Stynen created many pieces of furniture, halfway between craft and industrial production. These include a solid wood bench, the visible and large-sized holes creating an identity. It is a remarkable piece of furniture, the topicality of which really called for another edition.

When an architect like Léon Stynen is entrusted with designing furniture and lighting, we are faced with major, complete works.

Léon Stynen was also tasked with finding artists to decorate the inside of the building. Some of these were the teachers who surrounded him at the La Cambre school in Brussels. Later in this book Els Degryse describes their works, which in themselves constitute a collection of great artistic value.

The Ostend Kursaal, a major work by Léon Stynen, is the synthesis of architecture and design that offers much to please the sharp eyes of artists, spectators and visitors.

Kursaal 52 Oostende bench, re-edited by Leonet Hoang

Ostend Kursaal. A wooden seat in three colours of artificial leather, reflecting the ranges of light at the Kursaal. Hundreds of these seats filled these huge spaces.

The plywood technique is at the origin of free and elegant shapes. The creation of the SL 58 chair represents for Léon Stynen a new dimension. We are in 1958 and the World's Fair in Brussels is in preparation.

THIS CREATION IS SIGNIFICANT AND EXEMPLARY.

Function and materials offer Léon Stynen the bases of design. The maxim 'Function creates form' is so obvious here that even today nothing in the construction of this chair, and in particular nothing in the resulting use of the material can be perceived as gratuitous.

Léon Stynen's many architectural projects occupied all his creative spaces. The construction of his house on the shores of Lake Garda enabled him to design details for the private use of these spaces, but no other industrial projects of his saw the light of day. In this way, the SL 58 chair takes on a unique and essential importance in Léon Stynen's work.

In 2016, the Bulo brand undertook to reissue the original chair, still under the name SL 58, by adapting its proportions to the morphologies of humans in the 2000s. The components are faithful to the original 1958 model, that is plywood for the seat and curved steel for the feet. It is available in various woods and finishes – from natural wood and Santos rosewood to red or yellow lacquer. The chair can also be upholstered in cloth or leather.

The success of this edition both nationally and internationally quickly gave birth, under my direction, to an SLL 18 version which uses contemporary materials, such as polypropylene, to offer a lighter version of the SL 58 suitable for outdoor use and in a variety of colours to meet the demand for lively, joyful harmonies.
A chair is by nature the most dangerous exercise for a designer.

Architect Léon Stynen created a subtle osmosis between form, material and comfort. A butterfly, a cocoon, a poppy. All very simple. There is timelessness in this exercise.

A chair that is confidently a chair.

A chair with the modesty typical of Léon Stynen.

Today this chair demands respect for its variants.

For the SLL 18 we have in mind endless and uninhibited colour variations.
The freedom of excellence.

The SL 58 chair as re-edited by Bulo

The SLL 18 chair as re-edited by Bulo

ART &
THE KURSAAL

ELS DEGRYSE

Oscar Jespers, *The Four Winds,* 1955

Julien Van Vlasselaer, 1953

Edgard Tytgat, *The Embarkation of Iphigenia*, 1953 →

Paul Delvaux, 1952

Stynen opts for art: the Ostend Casino (Kursaal) as a *Gesamtkunstwerk*[1]

Background

Shortly after the Second World War, architect Léon Stynen (1899–1990) was commissioned to design a large new casino to replace the original building, which had been razed to the ground in 1940 by the German occupiers. The first traces of plans for a new Kursaal date back to the middle of the war. They are found in a letter by casino owner Gustave Nellens, dated 23 October and addressed to Stynen: 'I have returned from Ostend. The Kursaal is little more than rubble. It's important not to leave the ashes to cool too long.'[2] He then asked the architect to propose a design, seeing here an opportunity to build a third casino in Ostend in addition to those he owned in Knokke and Chaudfontaine. In 1944, the plans were complete and the duo was eager to move quickly after the war.[3] Eventually, the city organized a public competition and, on 26 June 1946, Stynen was notified that his design had won.[4] From that moment on, communication between Stynen and Nellens ceased and the architect's sole partner was the city. This was the start of a long and intense construction process that lasted until the official opening of the building on 20 June 1953. Covering an area of 1 hectare, the Kursaal was the largest casino in Europe at the time.

The building was widely acclaimed as a model of avant-garde modernism that was far ahead of its time. For example, Stynen connected the structure to the sea via large curved glass façades on the sea-facing side. The reinforced concrete skeleton, permitting non-load-bearing interior and exterior walls, was architecturally advanced. The architect was one of the first to use large aluminium windows, whose enormous dimensions were revolutionary at the time.

It is less known that the architect gave the Kursaal a striking artistic appearance by integrating high-quality art and decoration. Inspired by Henry van de Velde (1863–1957), the architect who preceded him as (first) director of La Cambre, the National Higher School for Decorative Arts, Stynen was keen to realize in Ostend his ambition to create a building as a veritable *Gesamtkunstwerk*. Like Van de Velde, he was imbued with the Bauhaus idea, in which the interaction between architecture, visual arts and crafts was obvious. To this end, he surrounded himself with a number of leading artists – many of them colleagues at La Cambre – and asked them to decorate the building. Today, the Kursaal is still decorated with sculptures by Oscar Jespers and George Grard, ceramics by Pierre Caille and Olivier Strebelle, a monumental frieze by Marc Mendelson, tapestry cartoons by Julien Van Vlasselaer and Edgard Tytgat, and stained-glass windows by Jo Maes, with the wall painting by Paul Delvaux as an absolute highlight.[5]

The struggle to integrate art

Even in his initial sketches, Stynen planned sculptures for various distinct places in the Kursaal. In the model he had made in 1944, the building is flanked by sculptures on both the seaward and landward sides, as well as on the large north-east staircase.[6] In his subsequently amended plans there were still three sculptures, two of them connected to the building and one sculpture on the dike. On the roof, Stynen had drawn a sculpture garden surrounded by walls as a sheltered place for sculptures.

He dreamed of an architectural promenade in the building, with works of art integrated in iconic places and culminating in a sculptural trail on the roof. Unfortunately, the city was not very supportive of this and Stynen had to adjust his plans several times. For example, the sheltered sculpture garden was replaced by a roof terrace on the west side of the building, which had little to do with Stynen's original plans. Nevertheless, he tried to integrate a sculpture garden on the terrace. He later made a concrete proposal to place five statues on the terrace by George Grard, Oscar Jespers, Henri Puvrez, Charles Leplae and Willy Kreitz.[7] Apart from the sculpture garden on the roof, the issue of integrating the three sculptures dragged on. In desperation, Stynen even proposed allocating his fees to pay for the integrated artworks.[8]

Despite all the opposition, Stynen stuck to his guns. A few months and many letters later, Stynen selected a number of artists with whom he wished to collaborate. He asked Oscar Jespers to design a sculpture for the canopy above the main entrance to the building. George Grard was allowed to make a sculpture for the seaward side and Henri Puvrez for the side of the bend in the dike known as Petit Nice. Finally, Willy Kreitz was responsible for the wall decoration.[9] However, no progress was made. In July 1951 the city refused any sculpture, with the exception of the wall decoration.

Shortly after the death of mayor Henri Serruys, on 25 January 1952, the tide suddenly seemed to turn. After five years of struggle, Stynen was given carte blanche to work with all the artists he had selected. In addition to the sculptures on the outside of the building, there would also be integrated artwork in the interior. He wrote to the city: 'The Kursaal should not only be a utilitarian building, but also a point of attraction due to the high quality of the works of art that are part of it.'[10]

Artists in the Kursaal

Julien Van Vlasselaer (1907–1982)
In his earliest architectural projects, Stynen already turned to Julien Van Vlasselaer to integrate art into his constructions. In 1944, he asked him to make colour drawings and gouaches of the design of the entire Kursaal interior.[11] These drawings were intended to be used for the presentation of the plans. Van Vlasselaer also designed a monumental cartoon for a tapestry in the Kursaal hall of honour. This cartoon, executed in seven vertical strips of paper glued together, was never turned into a tapestry and has hung in its original place since 1953.[12] It presents two personages, similar to playing card figures, representing the two aspects of the sea.

On the left, a fisherman's wife is tormented in her sleep by a storm; on the right, a woman enjoys the sun on the beach. The centre is dominated by a boat emerging between the waves, from which the anchor of hope is thrown. Van Vlasselaer played an important role in the renewed interest in tapestry weaving from the 1940s onwards. Mindful of the Bauhaus ideas, he was a fervent advocate for the integration of tapestry in architecture. His style is characterized by rhythmic compositions of shapes of ungraduated colours, stylized figures and increasingly abstract backgrounds. His cartoons are usually very colourful.

Oscar Jespers (1887–1970)

Oscar Jespers also appears very early in Stynen's design for the Kursaal. The artist and the architect both believed in the inseparable bond between sculpture and architecture. Jespers was also a pioneer in Belgium in the integration of sculpture. For him, sculpture served to extend the construction of the building: 'Monumental images attempt to be part of the building itself, without the slightest organic connection to or role in the construction.'[13] Even before the official architecture competition, Jespers was in contact with Stynen about a design for a sculpture. Stynen asked Jespers to come up with a monumental work for the canopy above the entrance to the building. It was to represent a synthesis of the 'three chief joys of life': air, light and water.[14] It eventually became *The Four Elements*: four beautiful, streamlined characters, harmoniously united as symbols for water, fire, earth and air. Placed on the entrance canopy, the impressive statue adds to the Kursaal's monumentality.

George Grard (1901–1984)

For the plinth on the Kursaal terrace, overlooking the sea, George Grard designed *The Sea*. The stylized body and hairstyle of this sensuous nude suggest the waves of the sea. Throughout his life, Grard remained true to his love for the female nude. Always working with live models, Isette Gabriels was his muse for *The Sea*. The sand-cast bronze sculpture is one of Grard's last monumental sculptures in which he emphasized the full, feminine form. Subsequently, he worked with a different female type, namely, a slim, elongated figure.

However, part of the Ostend public found the statue offensive. In fact, it was damaged shortly after its installation. When the vandalism continued, the city decided to move the statue to a park near the Leopold Park. To this day, the plinth still awaits its return.

Paul Delvaux (1897–1994)

The artistic jewel of the Kursaal is the monumental wall painting by Paul Delvaux, who also made a cartoon for a tapestry to decorate the interior. Incidentally, it was Henry van de Velde who suggested to Stynen that Delvaux be allowed to experiment on a large scale.[15] At the time, the latter was teaching monumental painting at the Brussels École de la Cambre. Stynen thus invited him to create a mural in the Kursaal, the first in a series of monumental works that would later follow. Not being sufficiently familiar with the technique of wall painting, Delvaux called on his lifelong friend Emile Salkin (1900–1977), a painter and teacher at the Tournai academy.

The wall that Stynen assigned to Delvaux was 26 metres long and 5 metres high. The composition is divided by painted columns. Delvaux placed tableaux between them in which a dark blue sky and a grey sea form a continuous horizon. In the central panel, a mermaid lies on her stomach in an armchair, a blue crown on her long wavy blonde hair. Her naked body contrasts with the solemn attire of the bourgeois women populating the rest of the composition.[16] In addition to the monumental wall painting, Delvaux also designed a cartoon for a tapestry intended for the hall of honour entitled *L'Annonce faite à Marie*, an unusual Annunciation scene with a naked Virgin Mary. The cartoon, in oil on canvas, has been lost. It probably was never hung in the Kursaal, nor made into a tapestry.

Pierre Caille, 1955

Pierre Caille, 1955

231

Marc Mendelson (1915–2013)
Another monumental wall painting in the Kursaal is the work of Marc Mendelson. This artist was also very interested in the relationship between architecture and painting. He had an instinctive feel for what shapes and colours an interior needed and how they should coincide with the space. In the early 1950s, his work evolved towards abstraction and the use of a more monochromatic colour palette. In the Kursaal, he produced a three-part frieze based on three colour tones – a key work in the evolution from figuration to abstraction. The frieze represents a wave movement that, as it were, offers a view out to the sea from the hall of honour. These large 'beach screens' were created with industrial resources, using synthetic dyes applied with a paint gun. The frieze is probably the first large wall-painting in Belgium to be done in this way.

Pierre Caille (1911–1996)
In addition to monumental wall paintings, Stynen also had important ceramic work integrated into the Kursaal. For this he turned to Pierre Caille, a pioneer of ceramic sculpture in Belgium. In 1950, the latter had developed a process for applying an inlay mosaic to architecture using stoneware plates. This technique appealed to Stynen and he invited Caille to realize several works in the Kursaal.[17] For the area above the stairs leading to the hall of honour, Caille designed a ceramic windshield covered with white enamel, incorporating cheerful fantasized marine motifs. Above the side exit to the building, he installed a sienna-coloured ceramic frieze with playful motifs like birds, waves and fish in white enamel. In the smoking room is a third ensemble of mosaic panels, consisting of a background of small black tiles with singing and dancing playing card-like figures. Finally, Caille designed two large dark female figures for the hall of honour with various colour areas consisting of tiles. They are clearly inspired by the major excursion he took through the Congo in 1949. Pierre Caille also worked together with a number of students in the Kursaal. For example, he had Iris Jasinski (1929–2016) make a ceramic horse for the entrance hall.

Olivier Strebelle (1927–2017)
For the concert hall, Stynen wanted to have two monumental works in dinanderie done by Henri Puvrez (1893–1971) and Oscar De Clerck (1892–1968).[18] However, he dropped that idea and asked Olivier Strebelle to make two ceramic works.[19] Strebelle designed *Triton*, a Neptune figure, and *Siren*, a mermaid.[20] Both monumental sculptures are in ceramic, finished in textured plaster with a scratched surface and stoneware glaze in muted colours.

Edgard Tytgat (1879–1957)
Edgard Tytgat made several designs for tapestries and Stynen asked him to create a cartoon for the Kursaal. Tytgat was well versed in history – from Greek mythology to biblical parables – and, as a pictorial storyteller, he mixed this cartoon with autobiographical elements. In his work, women are often the subject of kidnapping, beheading or execution. In *L'Embarquement d'Iphigenie*, a tapestry cartoon in oil on canvas, he depicted a story from Greek mythology, in which Iphigenia, the daughter of King Agamemnon, serves as a human sacrifice to enable the Greek fleet to continue on its way over becalmed seas. Tytgat portrayed the beautiful, desirable but condemned young woman in a subtly erotic way, with a touch of mischievous humour and in a fresh colour palette. The painting is one of the last series of scenes from the *Iliad* which Tytgat made before his death in 1957.[21]

Jo Maes (°1923)
With his glassware, Jo Maes is the only Ostend artist to have provided decorative work for the Kursaal. At the time, Maes was commissioned by architect Gaston Eysselinck (1907–1953) to make monumental ceramic reliefs and sandblasted glass scenes for the Ostend post office. Stynen probably learned about him from Eysselinck, given their acquaintance, and he liked the work. In the Kursaal reading room, there are seven stained-glass windows with abstract sea figures, four of them designed by Jo Maes and the three others by Emy De Cock.[22] She also contributed to the integration of art in the post-office building and produced a monumental wall-painting there.

The Kursaal, a monumental Gesamtkunstwerk
In the Kursaal, two aspects of Stynen come together in a remarkable way: his preference for classical architectural composition and his modernist ambitions, combining multiple branches of art. This is perhaps not surprising as he had trained in a Beaux-Arts tradition at the Royal Academy of Fine Arts in Antwerp, but was also imbued with the principles of Bauhaus. In his design for the Ostend Kursaal, he reconciled the two currents. Largely due to his approach to design as a *Gesamtkunstwerk,* he managed to produce a public building in which classicism and modernity merge. Stynen thought that the monumentality of the building should be perpetuated and enhanced by artistic interventions. He sought a form of monumentality that was concealed in a synthesis of architecture and visual art, thereby transcending the original functional aspects of the building. In the Kursaal, there is no additional visual and decorative work, but rather an intelligently realized confrontation of and interaction between architect, plastic artists and craftsmen. The integrated artwork gives meaning to the architecture and to the collective nature of the place.

Stynen did not limit his attention to integrating works of art, but also tried to leave his own mark on all the decoration in the building. In addition to the painting and decoration works (wall coverings, curtains, carpets, tapestries, door handles, lighting, plant boxes, flagpoles, stage settings, wood coverings, etc.), he also took on the design of the furniture. He was convinced that the building would not succeed if furniture and their furnishings were not in keeping with the overall design.[23] He personally designed the royal salon and the boxes for the royal couple and for the city council.[24]

With his *Gesamtkunstwerk* on the Ostend dike, Stynen achieved a new and unparalleled monumentality. The Kursaal can be regarded as one of the most successful examples of art integration in post-war architecture in Belgium.

The Kursaal was recognized in 1998 by the Department of Monuments and Landscapes of the Flemish Community for its cultural-historical value and is rightly protected as a heritage monument. In this way, one of the highlights of modernist architecture was saved from demolition.

1 This text is an extract from my master's thesis (*De geïntegreerde kunst in het Kursaal Oostende*, 2023), presented in the context of my Art studies at Ghent University. I therefore expressly wish to thank my adviser, Prof. Dr. Wouter Davidts, for supervising my thesis and the editing of this text.
2 Letter dated 23.10.1942 from Nellens to Stynen, VAi, Léon Stynen archive, Ostend file 3.1.352. With special thanks to Luc Laureys of the Stynen archive for his willing cooperation. All further quoted correspondence belongs to that archive.
3 Letter dated 21.01.1944 from Stynen to a certain Van Eeckhoven with the assignment to prepare a presentation of the plans. See also letter dated 27.09.1944 from Nellens to Stynen.
4 Letter dated 26.06.1946 from the City to Stynen.
5 A cartoon, derived from the Italian *cartone*, is a full-size working drawing, coloured in or not, that serves as a model for weaving a tapestry, or producing stained-glass windows, mosaics, etc. Such cartoons themselves are also highly valued as works of art.
6 Lode De Clercq, *Het Kursaal van Oostende: een hoogtepunt in de ontwikkeling van de monumentale kunst in België. Bijdrage tot de studie van het Kursaal-gebouw met het oog op de herwaardering en de restauratie,* unpublished study commissioned by architects Storme Van Ranst to mark the thorough renovation of 2000–04, p. 2.
7 Letter dated 26.05.1953 from Stynen to the City.
8 Letter dated 16.01.1950 from Stynen to the City.
9 Letter dated 28.02.1951 from Stynen to the City.
10 Letter dated 08.02.1952 from Stynen to the City.
11 Letter dated 07.03.1944 from Stynen to Van Vlasselaer.
12 The City hung the work in spring 1953 to show it to the general public during organized tours ahead of the official opening on 20 June 1953. Over the years, the work suffered serious damage, including water seepage and pigeon and gull droppings, resulting in drip marks, cracks, loss of fragments and gaps. In 2020, it was cleaned and thoroughly restored.
13 Oscar Jespers, 'Monumental sculpture', lecture given before the Royal Flemish Academy of Sciences, Letters and Fine Arts of Belgium, published in the *Mededelingen, Klasse der Schone Kunsten*, volume XII, 3 (1950), p. 12.
14 Letter dated 15.07.1947 from Stynen to the City.
15 Albert Bontridder, *La raison revoltée: Léon Stynen, sa vie et son œuvre / Gevecht met de rede: Léon Stynen, leven en werk*, Antwerp, Comité Léon Stynen, 1979, p. 108.
16 The mural was restored in 2021 after being quite severely damaged by water infiltration and impact damage from the intense use of the room. The restoration was carried out with respect for the original technique and materials. As a result, the painting looks fresh again, without compromising the natural ageing.
17 Rik Neven, *Met uitzicht op zee. Een nieuw begin voor het kursaal van Oostende*, Antwerp, Mercatorfonds, 2005, p. 53.
18 Letter dated 23.05.1952 from Stynen to the City. Dinanderie is a collective name for objects made of cast or beaten brass. The term refers to the city of Dinant, where many coppersmiths had their workshops. Monumental dinanderie was often used as decoration of buildings in this period.
19 Letter dated 08.08.1952 from Stynen to the City.
20 Both figures were removed from their places in the Kursaal during the major restoration campaign of 2000–04 and were hidden from public view for 20 years. Since 2021, they have been displayed in their place in the concert hall, supported by new concrete cantilever arms based on the original model.
21 The work was moved in the 1990s to Thermae Palace, the iconic spa hotel on the dike of Ostend. It has since been thoroughly restored and, since 2018, it once again adorns the Kursaal.
22 Letter dated 10.03.1953 from Stynen to the City. In 2021, the stained-glass windows were restored after breakage from impact. In consultation with the Immovable Heritage Department, invisible safety glass was placed in front of the windows. Lighting was also placed in the niches, so that indirect light falls on the glass windows and they come into their own.
23 Letter dated 14.10.1949 from Stynen to the City.
24 Letter dated 26.05.1953 from furniture and decoration company Galeyn to Stynen.

Marc Mendelson, 1953

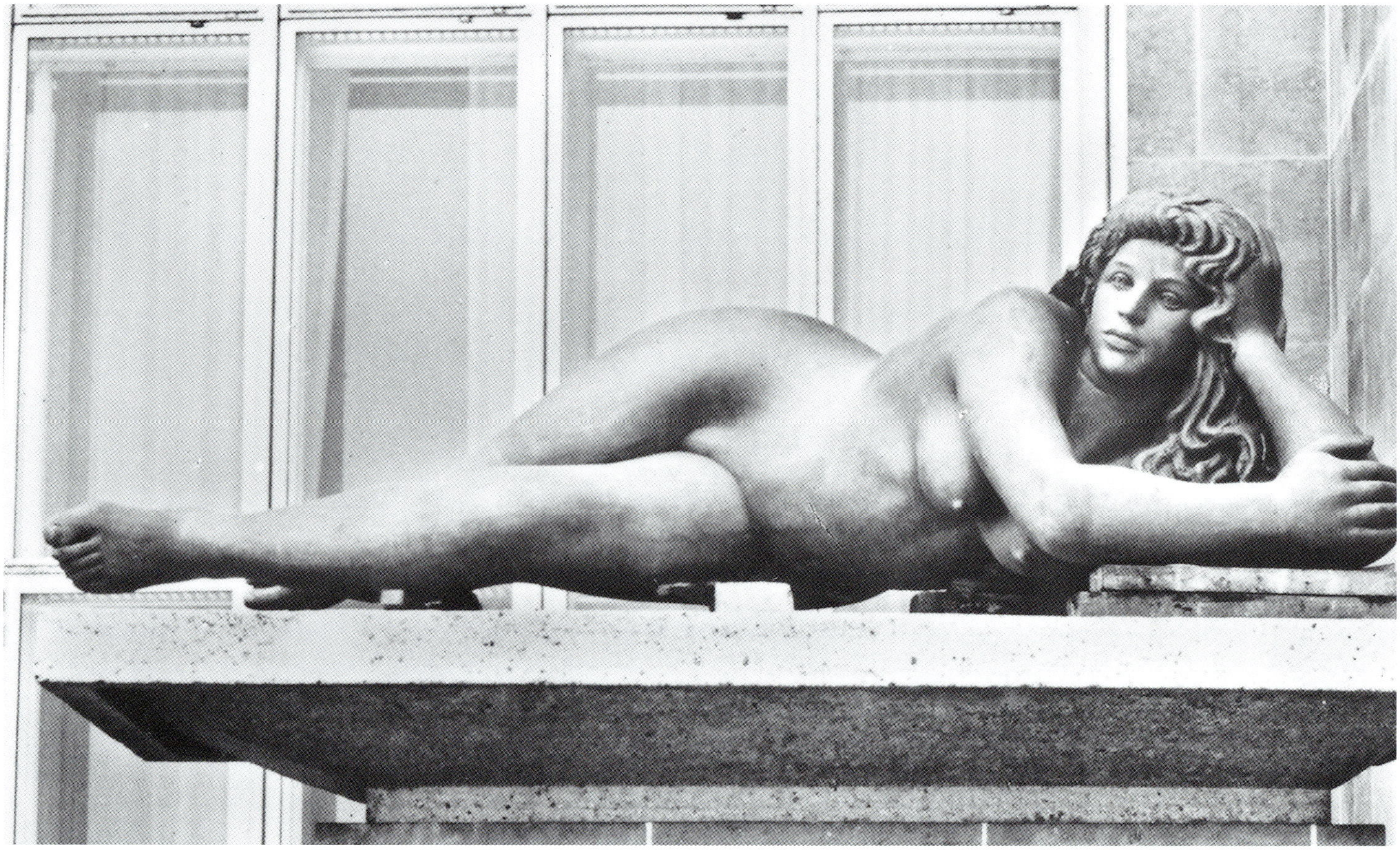

George Grard, *The Sea,* 1955

George Grard, *The Sea*, Leopold II laan, Ostend, 1955

Pierre Caille and pupils (incl. Iris Jasinski), 1955

Pierre Caille, 1955

Emy De Cock, 1953

Jo Maes, 1953

Olivier Strebelle, *Sirène*, 1953

Olivier Strebelle, *Triton*, 1953

ARCHITECTUUR

DE TROTS VAN OOSTENDE

Commercie en gebrek aan visie bedreigen het Oostends Kursaal en de Koninklijke Galerijen.

De Koninklijke Galerijen behoren ongetwijfeld tot de gaafste bouwwerken aan onze kust. Deze overdekte wandelgalerij met haar imposante zuilenrijen en bijhorende paviljoenen liet koning *Leopold II* in 1906 bouwen. Hiervoor deed hij een beroep op de befaamde en talentvolle Parijse architect *Charles Girault*. Dit uniek geheel is ondertussen erg verwaarloosd. Die schrijnende realiteit inspireerde schrijver *Eric De Kuyper*, die sinds kort terug in zijn geliefde Oostende woont, tot het formuleren van een zinvol voorstel (zie rubriek Boeken). Het project werd door de Koning Boudewijnstichting goedgekeurd en past in de Campagne Open Monumenten. De Kuyper wil de potenties die dit beschermd monument biedt, koppelen aan een culturele uitstraling, een idee dat aansluit bij de geest van wat Leopold II toentertijd voor ogen stond.

Het is een geschikte locatie voor een permanente tentoonstelling over het Oostende van rond de eeuwwisseling, en voor een klein filmcentrum waar met projecties de dimensie stad en toerisme kan worden opgeroepen. Het Filmmuseum in Brussel was enthousiast om het idee verder uit te werken. Tot zijn grote verbazing echter vernam De Kuyper dat het stadsbestuur al gekozen had voor een commerciële concessie. In een van de paviljoenen komt een *Interbrew*-horecazaak, genre *'t Zottekot* zoals in Antwerpen. Ook andere banaliserende attracties wil de stad een onderkomen geven in dit magistraal bouwwerk. Leopold II draait zich zeker om in zijn graf bij een dergelijk onzinnige aanwending van zijn geschenk aan Oostende.

Even dramatisch is het verloop van het Casino-Kursaal-dossier. In 1994 werd een wedstrijd georganiseerd die twee voorstellen opleverde waarbij het actueel gebouw van architect *Léon Stijnen* werd behouden. De wereldbefaamde Engelse bouwmeester *Sir Norman Foster* en de Belg *Bob van Reeth* daarentegen kozen voor een totaal nieuw complex. Toen het vorige stadsbestuur opteerde voor het voorstel van Van Reeth met een uitbouw in zee, ontstond er een ware storm van protest en werd alles afgevoerd.

HET LOBBYWERK WON

Dat het casino een dringende opknapbeurt moet krijgen, is voor iedereen duidelijk. De wijze waarop het stadsbestuur het gebouw wil „refunctionaliseren" tart echter elke verbeelding. Minister van Binnenlandse Zaken en raadslid *Johan Vande Lanotte* (SP) kan wel stellen dat „de impasse in het casinodossier na jaren is doorbroken", maar wat dit voor bedenkelijk resultaat zal opleveren, schat hij wellicht nauwelijks in. Zo is er voorzien dat een strook van vijftien meter van Stijnens gebouw aan de kant van de zeedijk wordt gesloopt en vervangen door een tien verdiepingen hoog appartementsgebouw. Het stadsbestuur hoopt dat de verkoop van de grond evenveel zal opleveren als de voorziene 780 miljoen frank die het renovatieproject zal kosten, iets wat zeer betwijfelbaar is.

Ondertussen werd tot 2034 een onderconcessie verleend aan *Flanders Eventhall* voor de uitbating van het kursaalgedeelte. Het contract met de groep *Verdonck* voor het casinogedeelte loopt tot 2014, op zich al een eigenaardige constructie.

De voorgestelde ruiloperatie bezit nog meer complicaties: het bestaande BPA-plan moet worden aangepast en bij de overeenkomst van 1873 kreeg het stadsbestuur het verbod om deze locatie te privatiseren.

Het voorstel is opgemaakt door *Restyling*, niet eens een architectenbureau, in samenwerking met het *Atelier d'Art Urbain* dat nauwe banden heeft met architect *Michel Jaspers*. Jaspers en Restyling maakten in 1994 ook een voorstel, een bar slecht ontwerp dat noch bij de jury noch bij de bevolking op enige appreciatie kon rekenen. Dat men nu opnieuw in zee gaat met deze equipe bewijst dat lobbywerk het haalt op een kwalitatieve benadering. Het feit dat het stadsbestuur kiest voor behendige jongens die modieuze maquillage-operaties bedenken, illustreert op welk laag niveau het beleid in Oostende is verzeild. Het ontbreken van massale publieke reactie op dit krankzinnig voorstel is verbazend. Is elk gevoel van trots in Oostende verdwenen?

Het wordt tijd dat er een „Koning Leopold II Stichting voor Architectuur en Stedebouw" wordt opricht die onmiddellijk Oostende ter verantwoording roept voor haar wandaden. Wanneer

De maquette van het Casino-Kursaal van Oostende: een koningin zonder kroon.

Oostende denkt met deze benadering haar internationale en toeristische uitstraling te kunnen opfrissen, dan vergist zij zich volledig. Het weinige kwalitatieve dat de eens zo geprezen Koningin der Badsteden nog bezit, wordt verkwanseld door een gebrek aan visie op langere termijn.

Marc Dubois

SOUTH ANTWERP
AN ENVIRONMENT

XAVIER DEWULF

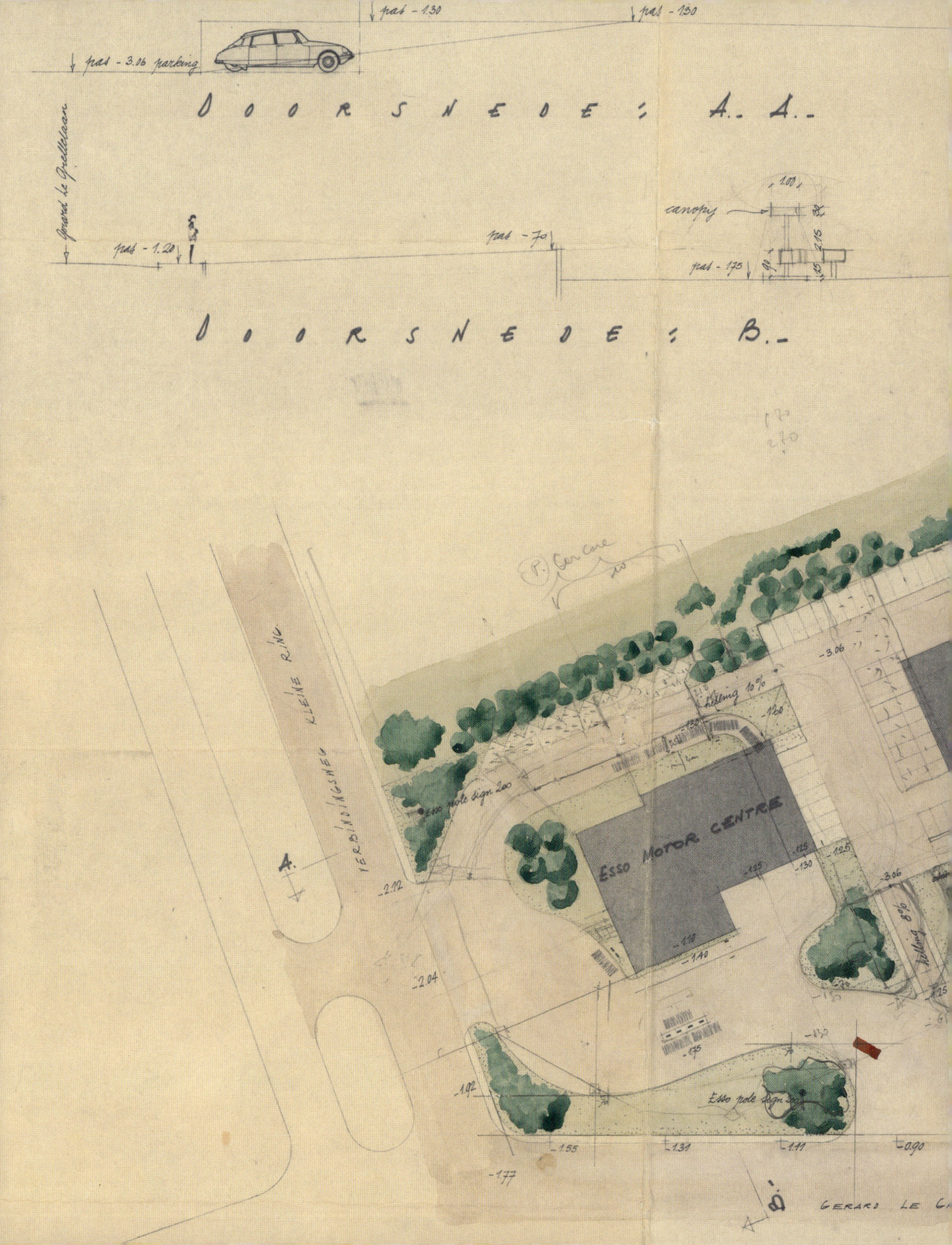

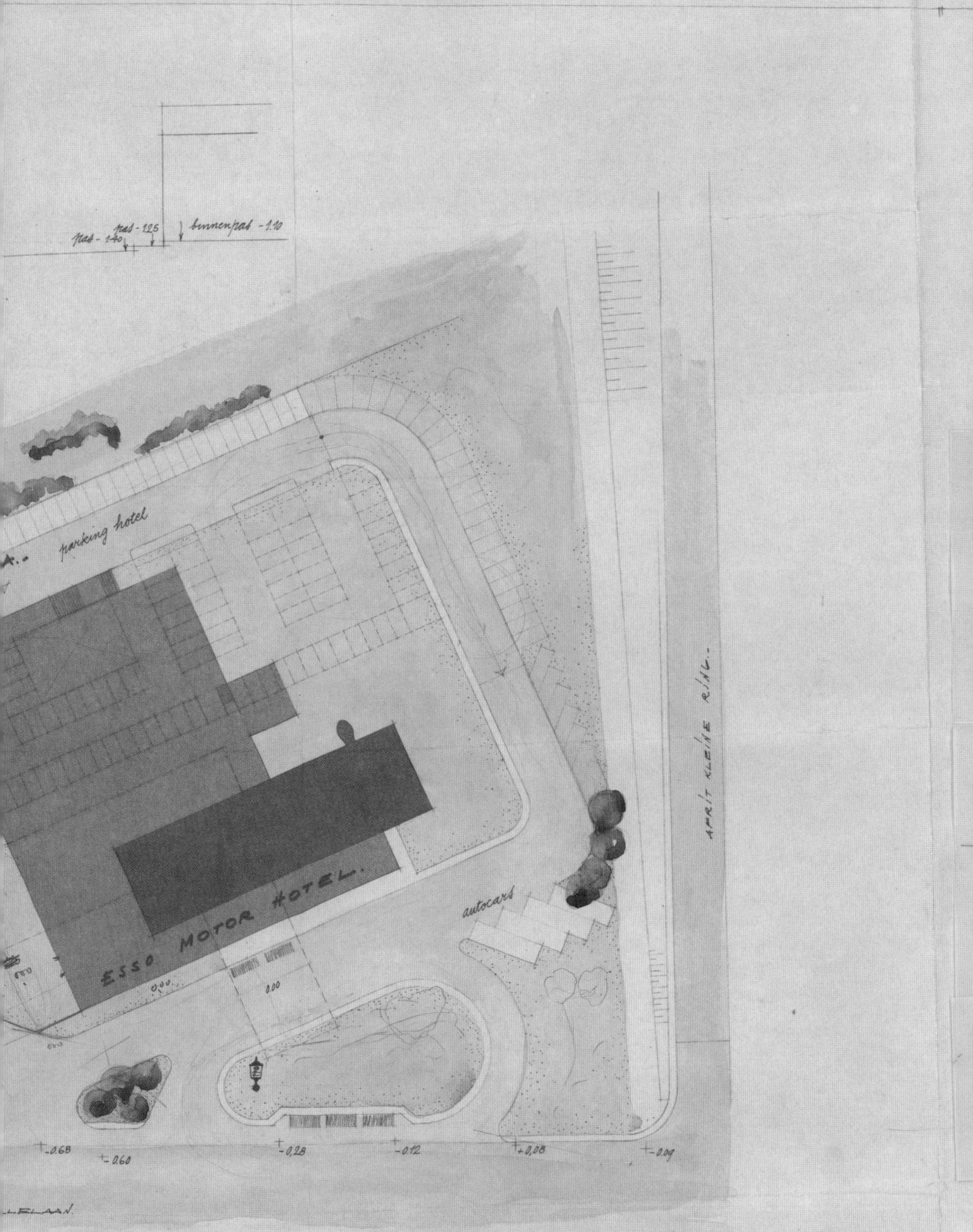

3D simulation

At the crossroads of modernity

A petrol station: the beating heart of modern society, bustling with life, accessible day and night, and representing everything and everyone.

Centrally located, Léon Stynen designed this fuel station to be a permanent connecting thread between the BP office building, the Esso Motor Hotel (now Crowne Plaza), and deSingel. This minimalist building also housed a busy garage, where lubricating oils flowed, for keeping cars roadworthy. Over the years, the garage fell into disuse. The building eventually became an Esso fuel station shop, which attracted more people, but most were just passing through. This lively place not only met man's material needs, but his inner needs – it was a symbolic space where dreams and reality converged. This purpose is embodied by the typical shapes and structures of the location.

In planning the future of the site, G&V Energy Group did not want to ignore this nod to the past. It therefore decided to completely renovate the building, paying due attention to the modernist icon's past, present, and future. Central to this process was therefore respecting what has been and what is yet to come. This place has afforded a warm welcome to everyone passing through since 1974. It had to be more than just a stop along the road or a monument by Léon Stynen. It needed to offer a genuine experience with a message, to be a beacon in Belgium's petroleum landscape.

Léon Stynen's original structures and ideas have been revered and now restored: from the contours of the building to the accents in the furniture and light fixtures, to the photography and atmospheric design.

The management of G&V Energy Group, led by CEO Xavier Dewulf, and its architect Ludo De Meester (Architecten Noord) have joined forces with Léon Stynen's granddaughter Tania Wolski to turn this unique location into an attraction for everyone. A place where forward-looking innovation and creativity unite with a veneration for the past, radiating not only a sense of nostalgia, but also soul.

Kursaal 52 Oostende bench, re-edited by Leonet Hoang

The SL 53 O light fitting as edited by Dark

PROJECTS, STUDIES AND COMPLETED CONSTRUCTIONS

1921–23	1914–18 war memorial – Knokke
1924	Project: 1914–18 war memorial in collaboration with sculptor G. Dumont – Antwerp
1924	Project: Open-air theatre. First prize in the triennial competition of the Royal Society of Architects – Antwerp
1924	House – Rue des Aduatiques 65, Brussels
1925	Comptoir Van der Elst, tobacconists – De Keyserlei, Antwerp
1927	Van den Bosch private residence – Kraainem
1927–28	Verstrepen private residence – Antwerpsestraat 134, Boom
1928	Project: Residence for the Governor of Léopoldville – Congo
1929	Project: Scheldt tunnel – Antwerp
1930	Decorative Arts Pavilion at the Antwerp World's Fair
1930	De Beukelaer Pavilion at the Antwerp World's Fair
1930	Knokke Casino
1930–31	Double holiday home – Koninklijke Baan, Nieuwpoort
1931	Dr. Nyssen private residence – Lozanastraat, Antwerp
1931	Project: Naval Academy – Ostend
1932	Project: Mohanlal House – Bombay, India
1932	Blankenberge Casino in collaboration with R. Speybrouck and G. Van Sluys
1932	MEGA shops and offices – Hasselt
1933	Verheyden private residence – Antwerp
1933	Apartment building on a green site in Elsdonck – Antwerp
1933	Study for a Scheldt bridge – Antwerp
1933	Van Parijs private residence – Schoten
1935	Cinema Rex – Antwerp
1935	Six single-family dwellings – Linkeroever, Antwerp
1935	Salti private residence – Blokskesweg, Kapellen
1935	Lachapelle apartment building – Lodewijk Gerritslaan, Berchem-lez-Anvers
1935	Project: INR building, Place Flagey, Brussels, in collaboration with A. Portielje and J. De Braey
1936	Dr. Van Thillo private residence – Ekeren
1936	De Beukelaer country house – Brasschaat
1936	Dr. Koumans private residence – Koningshof, Schoten
1936	Douchar private residence – Koningin Astridlaan, Hasselt
1937	Sanatorium – Brasschaat
1937	Van Eycklei duplex apartments – Antwerp
1937	Housing complex – Britselei, Antwerp
1938	Fitting out of the liner *Baudouinville*
1938	Fitting out of the ferry *Prince Philip*
1938	Lobby, Eldorado Cinema - Brussels
1938	Chaudfontaine Casino
1939	Belgian Pavilion at the New York World's Fair, in collaboration with H. van de Velde and V. Bourgeois
1939	Sources de Chaudfontaine Pavilion – International Water Exhibition, Liège
1939	Fitting out of fisheries control vessel *Artevelde*
1941	M. Vereecke private residence with offices – Strijdhoflaan, Berchem
1941	Wine warehouse for Elias – Godefriduskaai, Antwerp
1942	Baron Opsomer private residence in collaboration with P. Smekens – Maria-Theresialei, Antwerp

1942	Dwellings for the Antwerp Docks company – Frilinglei, Brasschaat
1942	Urban planning study for the municipality of Brasschaat
1944	Project: Industrial and office buildings for the Lint company – Kontich
1944–53	Casino-Kursaal – Ostend
1945	Project: 3,000 emergency homes to be built on land in Linkeroever, Antwerp
1945	Soap factory – Leuven
1946	Fitting out of the liner *MS Batory* for Poland
1947	Workshop and showroom for the Chrysler automobile company – Haringrodestraat, Antwerp
1947	La Métropole printing works – Lombardenvest, Antwerp
1948	Excelsior printing works for the *Volksgazet* newspaper – Antwerp
1948	Higher State Technical Institute, in collaboration with M. Wynants – Leopoldstraat, Mechelen
1948	Offices for the Wuyts company – Blindestraat, Antwerp
1948	Van der Elst private residence – Gabriëllelei, Brasschaat
1948	Urban planning study for the municipality of Schoten (survey and development plan)
1948	Three projects: Transformation and major redevelopment of the Academy of Fine Arts – Mutsaertplein, Antwerp
1949	Project: Institute for Architecture and Urban Planning – Linkeroever, Antwerp
1949	Petrol station – Franklin Rooseveltplein, Antwerp
1950	Mining School, in collaboration with G. De Hens and M. Van Isacker – Hasselt
1950	Taeymans private residence – Frilinglei, Brasschaat
1951	Consulate of the United States of America – Antwerp
1952	Transaf office building – Lange Klarenstraat, Antwerp
1953	Maes country house – Palmenlaan 10, Antwerp
1953	Fitting out of the cabins of the Ostend-Dover ferry
1953	Office building for the Albatross company – Antwerp
1953	Showroom, offices and workshop of the Établissements Moorkens – Grote Steenweg 571, Berchem
1954	De Zonnewijzer residential and office complex – Mechelsesteenweg 247, Antwerp
1954	Pâtisserie Schoenaers – Belgiëlei 101, Antwerp
1955	Villa Luft, Kapellen
1955	Social housing – Kessel-Lo
1955	La Belgo-Luxembourgeoise office building – corner of Rue Belliard and Rue d'Arlon, Brussels
1955	Fitting out of the channel ferry *King Leopold III*
1956	Project: Brussels administrative centre, in collaboration with H. Van Kuyck, the Alpha group, M. Lambrichs and G. Riquier (Stynen quit the team in 1958)
1956	Project: Development of Place Rogier, Brussels
1956	Office building for a mining company - Antwerp
1956	Housing complex – one 120-apartment building and 80 individual houses – Prins-Regentplein, Kessel-Lo
1956	Primary school and kindergarten – Kessel-Lo
1957	Fitting out of the car ferry *Artevelde*
1958	Lobby of the Grand Palais V at the Brussels World's Fair
1958	Petroleum Enterprises Pavilion at the Brussels World's Fair
1958	Liebig Pavilion at the Brussels World's Fair
1958	Industrial design: series featuring a chair, a door handle and a door push
1958	Project: bridge over the Alzette – Luxembourg
1958	Uccle cultural and artistic centre – Rue Rouge, Brussels

1958	Office building for the Sociétés réunies d'énergie du bassin de l'Escaut (EBES) – Antwerp
1958	Bureau Veritas headquarters – Uitbreidingstraat 392, Berchem
1959	Telex building – Boulevard de l'Impératrice 19, Brussels
1959	EBES office building, in collaboration with H. Van Kuyck – Mechelsesteenweg 271, Antwerp
1959–63	Belgium Petroleum headquarters – Jan Van Rijswijcklaan 16, Antwerp
1960	Administrative and technical centre for the Régie des télégraphes et téléphones (RTT) – Brussels
1960–62	Assurance liégeoise office building – Frankrijklei 70, Antwerp
1961–63	Metallen Galler company, shop and offices – Italiëlei 22-24, Antwerp
1962	Project: Glaverbel S.A. headquarters – Brussels
1962–72	Urban planning study Wezenberg – Antwerp
1962–87	Royal Music Conservatory Antwerp – Jan Van Rijswijcklaan, Antwerp
1963	C&A clothing store – Meir 66, Antwerp
1963	Stynen-Degrez private house – Lake Garda, Italy
1963	BMW complex – Chaussée de Charleroi 123, Brussels
1963	Urbanization project for a residential area in central Antwerp
1963	Design of the Amsterdam-Paris TEE train
1963–64	C&A clothing store – Demerstraat 11-15, Hasselt
1963–65	C&A clothing store – Rue Neuve, Brussels
1964	Brachfeld-CBS diamond-cutting workshop and offices – Hofstraat, Antwerp
1964	Peter Pan primary and secondary school – Rue des Pierres 11-13, Brussels
1964	Project: Administrative Centre for the Province of Brabant
1965	Project: Ghent cultural and economic centre
1965	Transformation of the Belvedere Palace – Brussels
1965–66	C&A clothing store – Ghent
1966	St Rita's pilgrimage church – Harelbeke
1966	Transformation of the Diamond Bourse – Antwerp
1966	Arpic/Atlas Copco social services – Wilrijk
1966	Project: Museum of Modern Art to be built near the Steen – Antwerp
1966	Stynen-Wolski private residence – Chaussée de Bruxelles 94, La Hulpe
1966–67	C&A clothing store – Kortrijk
1967–69	C&A clothing store – Charleroi
1967–72	Riverside Tower apartment building – Linkeroever, Antwerp
1968	Kredietbank – Antwerp
1968	ASLK office building – Antwerp
1969	C&A clothing store – Namur
1969	President Building, offices – Franklin Rooseveltplein, Antwerp
1969	Regional offices of the CGER/ASLK – Antwerp
1969–70	C&A clothing store – Bruges
1970	Esso Motor Hotel – Verbindingsweg, Antwerp
1970	Project: Museum of Modern Art in collaboration with Le Corbusier and A. Wogenscky – Middelheim Park, Antwerp
1970	Project: Shopping centre in Antwerp
1973	Administrative offices of the National Office for Annual Holidays (ONVA/RJV) – Brussels
1973	Supermarket GB Inno shopping centre – Wijnegem
1974	Extension of GB supermarket and car park – Groenplaats, Antwerp -
1975	Administrative building – Chaussée d'Ixelles, Brussels

Sources: Albert Bontridder, *La raison révoltée: Léon Stynen, sa vie et son oeuvre / Gevecht met de rede: Léon Stynen, leven en werk*, Antwerp, Comité Léon Stynen, 1979

AUTHORS' BIOGRAPHIES

Anne Stynen, born in Antwerp in 1938, began her studies at La Cambre in 1957. She learned bookbinding in the workshop of Professor Vladimir Tchékéroul. After working for many years in Brussels in silk-screen printing and communication in the design and fashion sector, she moved to Venice in 1983. She currently resides in Brescia, Italy.

Tania Wolski was born in Brussels in 1964. A sculptress, creator of installations and interactive experiences, she actively and harmoniously mixes traditionally distant disciplines. She is also a consultant in conceptualization, process development and management, and risk and financial analysis.

Following a doctorate in political science at the university of Padua, she occupied various management functions, including representing craft workers and small and mid-size enterprises (SMEs) in the Venice region to the European Union. Today, she utilizes her combined talents to serve both SMEs and multinationals, while continuing to pursue her artistic career.

Sophie Wolski was born in Brussels in 1966. She has lived in Italy since the 1980s, where she obtained a doctorate in political science. After spending several years organizing a theatre and poetry festival for the Teotro Due Foundation from Parma and heading the teaching department of the CSAC (Centro Studi e Archivio della Comunicazione) of the same city, she is currently responsible for organizing the ParlaJazz Frontiere festival.

Marc Dubois (°1950) is an architect, art historian and senior lecturer, Faculty of Architecture KULeuven in Ghent and Brussels until 2015. Curator of various exhibitions, including the *Venice Architectural Biennale* 1991 (Belgian pavilion). Curator for the International INTERIEUR Biennale 1996 and 1998 in Kortrijk. Since 1992, adviser for the Mies van der Rohe Award in Barcelona. Awarded the ULTIMA prize (2019) of the Flemish Community. Honorary Fellow (2021) of the Royal Institute of British Architects (RIBA). From 2015 to 2022, chair of DOCOMOMO Belgium.

Since 1996, correspondent for *casabella*. Author of books on the work of architects Albert Van huffel, Álvaro Siza, Philippe Samyn, Vincent Van Duysen and Bart Lens. Author of *Tendenze dell' architettura contemporanea – Belgio Architettura gli ultimi vent'anni*, Electa, 1993. And the Monograph *Gaston Eysselinck 1907–1953. In the Footsteps of Le Corbusier*, Snoeck, 2019.

Pablo Lhoas
Architect (La Cambre 1989 – Marcel Pesleux's studio), in practice since 1990.
Together with his brother Pierre Lhoas from 1992, he established a practice that focuses on renovation and combines various categories of architecture (furniture/scenographies/domestic, cultural and school programmes, etc.) in an eclectic, curious, experimental and essentially hyperfunctionalist mode.

Since 1995, Pablo Lhoas has taught at the Higher Institute of Architecture of the French Community La Cambre, which merged in 2009 with the Higher Institute of Architecture Victor Horta. They formed the Faculty of Architecture La Cambre Horta of the Free University of Brussels in the fields of architectural design, history and criticism. Lhoas was Dean of the Faculty of Architecture between 2016 and 2022. He is currently director of the École nationale supérieure d'architecture et de paysage in Lille.

An 'activist' by nature, Pablo Lhoas is co-author with Jean-Louis Genard of *Qui a peur de l'architecture? Livre blanc de l'architecture contemporaine en Communauté française de Belgique* (La Lettre volée / ISACF – La Cambre, 2004) and initiator or co-initiator of several public campaigns relating to the culture, politics and history of architecture and urban planning, including recently the demand to conserve Léon Stynen's C&A building in Namur.

Luc Vincent was born on 22 January 1952 in Brussels, son of an architect father and a haute couture designer mother. Both were students at the La Cambre school. After a somewhat erratic general education, he discovered in Christophe Gevers a master in design and interior architecture.

A graduate of La Cambre, Vincent is the author of numerous projects for, among others, Bulo, Modular, Hind Rabii, Serax, Pantone, Tecno, Totem, and Dark and directs the design units of the architecture firms of Ricardo Bofill and Jean Nouvel.

This book, *Léon Stynen, Architect*, is for him a first step towards other experiences. He wishes to thank the members of the Stynen family for putting their trust in him.

Els Degryse (°1971) holds a law degree (KULeuven, 1994) with a specialization in environmental law (Fondation Universitaire Luxembourgeoise, 1995). She worked for ten years as a lawyer at the Bruges Bar. She then decided to follow her heart and switched to the cultural sector. Since 2003, she has worked as a staff member in the Ostend Kursaal. In 2023, she will graduate with a master's in the arts and sciences (Ghent University). Her master's thesis examines the integrated art in the Ostend Casino (Kursaal).

Xavier Dewulf is the CEO of G&V Energy Group, a Belgian company which is growing rapidly in the field of fuel distribution and charging stations for electric cars.

G&V Energy Group operates more than 27 centres in Brussels, Hainaut and Flanders, and manages more than 200 fuel stations under its own brand and other well-known names (Esso, Shell, Total and Q8).

In connection with G&V Energy Group's expansion in this area, it recently acquired the emblematic fuel station in Antwerp designed by Léon Stynen.

THE PHOTOS AND THEIR AUTHORS

© Archive Stynen-Wolski unless otherwise stated

covers	photo EPMC
	© Bulo, Eugeen Vangroenweghe (Verne)
24	*below, right* © Marc Sels
25	© Marc Sels
31	© Tania Wolski
52	© Tania Wolski
53	© Tania Wolski
55	© C. Bender
56	© D'hont
57	*below* © D'hont
58	© D'hont
	© Antony d'Ypres
59	*below* © D'hont
66–67	© Vlaams Architectuurinstituut – Collection Vlaamse Gemeenschap, archive Léon Stynen
71	*below* © Malevez
73	*below* © Vlaams Architectuurinstituut – Collection Vlaamse Gemeenschap, archive Léon Stynen
74–79	© Vlaams Architectuurinstituut – Collection Vlaamse Gemeenschap, archive Léon Stynen
80	© Remy Bauters
81	© Willy Bosschem
82–83	© Pierre Tombeur
90–91	© Ian Segal
95	*above* © Pierre Tombeur
96–101	© Vlaams Architectuurinstituut – Collection Vlaamse Gemeenschap, archive Léon Stynen
105	*below* © Guy Croegaert
116–117	© SABAM Belgium 2023
119	© SABAM Belgium 2023
124	Archive Marc Dubois, Gent © SABAM Belgium 2023
126	*above* © Vlaams Architectuurinstituut – Collection Vlaamse Gemeenschap, archive Léon Stynen and Paul De Meyer © SABAM Belgium 2023
	middle Archive Marc Dubois, Gent © Gaston Eysselinck
	below Archive Marc Dubois, Gent
127	Design Museum Gent, Archive Eysselinck © Gaston Eysselinck
128	Archive Marc Dubois, Gent © W.M. Dudok
129	© Vlaams Architectuurinstituut – Collection Vlaamse Gemeenschap, archive Léon Stynen and Paul De Meyer
130	Archive Library CIVA, Brussels
131	Archive Marc Dubois, Gent
133	© Vlaams Architectuurinstituut – Collection Vlaamse Gemeenschap, archive Léon Stynen and Paul De Meyer
135	© Vlaams Architectuurinstituut – Collection Vlaamse Gemeenschap, archive Léon Stynen © Marc Dubois
136	© Vlaams Architectuurinstituut – Collection Vlaamse Gemeenschap, archive Léon Stynen and Paul De Meyer © Marc Dubois
138	© Vlaams Architectuurinstituut – Collection Vlaamse Gemeenschap, archive Léon Stynen
139	*left* © Vlaams Architectuurinstituut – Collection Vlaamse Gemeenschap, archive Léon Stynen *right* © Kenzō Tange © Marc Dubois
140	*left* © Corneille Hannoset *right* © © Vlaams Architectuurinstituut – Collection Vlaamse Gemeenschap, archive Léon Stynen
143	
146	© Marc Dubois
147	© H. Kessels
148	© Fonds Lucien De Roeck Archive Stynen-Wolski © Fonds Lucien De Roeck
149	© Fonds Lucien De Roeck
150	© H. Kessels *above* © Haine Broers
151	*below, left* © H. Kessels
200	*above* © H. Kessels *above* © Vlaams Architectuurinstituut – Collection Vlaamse Gemeenschap, archive Léon Stynen
201	
203	© Design Museum Gent
205	© Tania Wolski
207	© Hilde Van Cauwelaert, archive Kursaal Oostende
208	© Luc Vincent
210	© Tijs Vervecken
211	© Tijs Vervecken © René Guiette
212–214	© Tijs Vervecken
215	© Bulo, Eugeen Vangroenweghe (Verne) © Bulo, Eugeen Vangroenweghe (Verne) *beeld* © Tania Wolski
216	© Tania Wolski
217	© Tania Wolski
218–221	© Tania Wolski
224	© Oscar Jespers © Pieter Clicteur
225	© Julien Van Vlasselaer © Pieter Clicteur
226	© Edgard Tytgat © Damon De Backer
230	© SABAM Belgium 2023 © Damon De Backer © Damon De Backer
231	© Pierre Caille © Damon De Backer © Pierre Caille © Damon De Backer
235	© Pierre Caille © Pieter Clicteur
236	© Marc Mendelson © Pieter Clicteur Archive George Grard © George Grard
237	© George Grard © Pieter Clicteur © Pierre Caille & Iris Jasinski © Pieter Clicteur
238	© Pierre Caille © Pieter Clicteur © Pierre Caille © Pieter Clicteur © Emy De Cock © Steve Dinneweth © Jo Maes © Steve Dinneweth
239	*above* © Olivier Strebelle © Steve Dinneweth © Damon De Backer
240	© Pieter Clicteur
241	© Knack 1997
244–245	© Vlaams Architectuurinstituut – Collection Vlaamse Gemeenschap, archive Léon Stynen
246	© Ludo De Meester, Noord Architecten
248	© Leonet Hoang
249	© Serge Vandercam

LÉON STYNEN ARCHITECT

Editors: **Luc Vincent, Tania Wolski**
Authors: **Els Degryse, Xavier Dewulf, Marc Dubois, Pablo Lhoas, Anne Stynen, Luc Vincent, Sophie Wolski, Tania Wolski**
Copy-editing: **Christopher Reid**
Proofreading: **Duncan Brown**
Translation: **Michael Lomax**
Graphic design: **Jean-Michel Meyers**
Printing: **Printer Trento**, Italy

Titles font: **LUCIEN** by Lucien De Roeck, 1934

Snoeck Publishers
Director: **Philip Van Bost**
Publisher: **Gunther De Wit**

© Snoeck Publishers, Ghent, 2023
© all authors and photographers, 2023

ISBN 978-9-4616-1756-9
Legal deposit: D/2022/0012/60

Thanks to:
Hilde Van Cauwelaert, Wouter Davidts, Damon De Backer, Fonds Lucien De Roeck, Steve Dinneweth, Chantal Grard, Leo Van Hoorick (Autoworld), Dirk Laureys (VAi), Magda de Meester & Paul Clerinx, Ian Segal, Marnick Smessaert, Geert-Jan Van Cauwelaert, Eva Van Regenmortel (Design Museum Gent), Tijs Vervecken

All rights reserved. No part of this publication may be reproduced or transmitted in any form or by any means, electronic or mechanical, including photocopy, recording or any other information storage and retrieval system, without prior permission in writing from the publisher. Every effort has been made to contact copyright-holders of illustrations. Any copyright-holders whom we have been unable to reach or to whom inaccurate acknowledgment has been made are invited to contact the publisher.